"If you are a Christian who wants to  THIS BOOK. With powerful insi marketplace, Rebranding Christiani from being respected, to tolerated, to canceled in a few short decades. Better yet, these pages reveal how to turn the tide and get our focus and branding back in alignment with Jesus's message and our calling as his ambassadors."

—LARRY OSBORNE,
Author & Pastor
North Coast Church

"Rebranding Christianity starts where the gospel starts, with grace, love, and a call to change for people who often fall short. But this is not an easy book to read. It is honest about where the church is and how it has come up short in what, and, more importantly, who it claims to represent. The book argues in practical detail for another way that is better in touch with Jesus' heart and actions, the one who died for us while we were yet sinners. This book will help you recover that focus. In the rebranding, with a wedding of grace, love, and a changed way of relating, the people of God can better represent the heart of the God they love."

—DARRELL BOCK,
Executive Director for Cultural Engagement, Howard G. Hendricks Center for Christian Leadership and Cultural Engagement. Senior Research Professor of New Testament Studies, Dallas Theological Seminary

"I think the evangelical church is in trouble, in fact, I'm skeptical it will survive the next generation. I agree with Jeff Jones, the solution is going back to the admonition that was left, to the practice that permeated the early church, to… well stop reading this and start reading the book, it's really good and it points us in the right direction."

—PETE BRISCOE,
Executive Coach and Host of the Kindavangelical Podcast

"The message of Jesus Christ is the greatest and most triumphant message we will ever encounter. One can see from the trajectory of the culture, that many no longer think of it as relevant, impactful or life-changing. In this thought-provoking book Jeff uses an ingenious approach to compare the brand of Christianity to other successful brands. As a result, readers will walk away enticed by a renewed perspective of what it means to represent the brand of Jesus Christ well."

—JADA EDWARDS,
Author and Bible Teacher

"American Christianity is at an important turning point, and this book will help move the church toward a much-needed correction back to the original brand as given by our Founder. Jeff has effectively led a next paradigm church for decades that is changing the perception of Christianity in his own community and therefore serves as a reliable guide to help move us to a better place."

—STEVE STROOPE,
Founding Pastor of Lakepointe Church

"Rebranding Christianity is a compelling and timely perspective on the American church and how we, as church leaders and everyday Christians, can rebuild Christianity's reputation. Jeff, Mike, and Dwight build an insightful biblical and business case that is critical for every church leader to embrace moving into the future."

—KADI COLE,
Leadership Consultant, Executive Coach, and
Author of *Developing Female Leaders*

"When you lose your way, you need a guide to get you headed back in the right direction. I can't think of a better person to guide us than my dear friend, Jeff Jones. Rebranding Christianity lays out a practical way for each of us to see the real heart of Jesus for all people. This book will change your thinking and challenge you to reach others in a deeper, more meaningful way. This book is the start of something new – an encouraging guide that could be just what we need to make the American Church fruitful again."

—PATRICK KELLEY,
Founding and Senior Pastor of River Pointe Church

"Rebranding Christianity creates a conversation I believe every Christian leader should be having with their teams and churches. This book did a phenomenal job of not just stating the problem but providing clear and practical solutions for how Jesus followers can win over a skeptical world."

—RYAN LEAK,
Executive Coach and Best-Selling Author, *Chasing Failure*

If the word "brand" throws you off, take another look. Far from a manual on marketing Christianity, Jones and his fellow authors call Christians to recover the heart of Jesus's message, and the ultimate evidence for Christianity's truth, unconditional love for others. If you struggle to hold on to hope in the future of Christianity in America, read this book to face our failures, discern root causes, and to discover hope for a better future in the power of God—if we make crucial changes. Read this book and give it to a friend!

—BRUCE B. MILLER,
Senior Pastor, Christ Fellowship
Author, *Leading a Church in a Time of Sexual Questioning*

"Rebranding Christianity is a work for our time, a time in which spiritual curiosity remains high despite mounting struggles with the current "brand" of Christianity. Jeff is a student of culture as much as he is a student of Scripture, and the innovative approach he, Mike, and Dwight take in going well beyond naming the self-inflicted challenges facing the faith community to offering practical wisdom and corrective steps offer a roadmap for the American church in the coming decade."

—JASON WILLIAMS,
Executive Pastor of Ministries, Saddleback Church

"Jeff powerfully addresses the mistake of resorting to culture war in divisive times. It always ends in ugly behavior and damage to the gospel. Many years later, there will be deep regret and passionate apologies for past mistreatment of people. So, why even go there? Jeff convincingly calls us to a more difficult discipleship path. A more genuine following of Jesus. A more authentic abiding in the True Vine. A path of engaging, serving, and loving others so well that they see Jesus in us!"

—BILL HENSON
President, Posture Shift Ministries (postureshift.com)
Author, *Guiding Families of LGBT+ Loved Ones* (guidingfamilies.com)

"A few years back, when faced with the perfect storm of a pandemic, racial tensions, and a polarized presidential election, our country was blown far away from whatever Christian roots had existed." We pastors struggled to know how to respond and more importantly, how to lead the church through this storm. So, with the skill of both a church practitioner and the insight of a biblical scholar, Jeff Jones offers practical and time-tested solutions that will help pastors navigate through these ongoing difficult times. As a friend and a fellow pastor, I've watched Jeff live and lead what he teaches, and pastors and church leaders will benefit greatly from considering and utilizing Jeff's teachings. And personally, I look forward to leading others through the principles laid out in Rebranding Christianity."

—DR. DAVID ASHCRAFT,
Pastor Emeritus, LCBC Church; President and Founder, The Advantage;
Author, *What Was I Thinking?*

People who were nothing like Jesus liked Jesus, and he liked them back. But the same can't be said for Jesus followers today. And that's a problem. Jeff brings a unique perspective on how Christians can use a 21st century approach to clearly reflect what is already true about Jesus' irresistible gospel. It's a must-read for pastors, followers of Jesus, and anyone who longs to recapture the power behind Jesus' message from two millennia ago.

—ANDY STANLEY,
Author, Communicator, and Senior Pastor of North Point Ministries

REBRANDING
CHRISTIANITY

When the World's Most Important Brand Loses Its Way

Jeff Jones

with Mike Hogan and Dwight Jewson

Cover Design by Mackenna Cotten

Published in association with The Fedd Agency, Inc., a literary agency.

Fedd Books
P.O. Box 341973
Austin, TX 78734

www.thefeddagency.com

ISBN: 978-1-957616-39-1
eISBN: 978-1-957616-40-7

LCCN: 2023906679

First Edition

Printed in the United States of America

TABLE OF CONTENTS

INTRODUCTION

I've been a pastor for over thirty years, and I feel a cultural change. I bet you do too. Christianity used to be respected. People felt like they should attend church even if they didn't. Pastors were revered, even called "Reverend" at times. Those days are long gone.

As a pastor, the most dreaded question I field from strangers I'm seated next to on a plane or paired up with for a golf round is, "So what do you do?" When I respond with, "pastor," the conversation is shut down so quickly and awkwardly that I think it might be better to lie—to say anything else. Even "axe murderer" might go over better because at least it might elicit some curiosity: "So, how did you get into that line of work?" or, "What kind of axe do you prefer?"

You may remember the days when *Christian* meant somebody better than you. I became a Christian as a young teenager in the early eighties and began to date a Christian girl from my youth group. My non-believing friends gave me a hard time: "Oh, a Christian girl? Don't you think she's a little too good for you?" If this same situation happened today, my friends would probably say, "Really? A Christian girl? Yuck! Why would you date her?" Nowadays, Christians seem to be portrayed as worse than everyone else. Christians who were once seen as the good people—even too good—are now viewed as the worst of humanity.

This trend began before 2020, but the COVID-19 pandemic accelerated the change faster than anybody could have predicted. The perfect storm of a pandemic, racial tensions, and a polarized presidential election blew our country far away from whatever Christian roots existed. We will discuss this perfect storm more deeply later. Add to that the ethical failures of some prominent Evangelical leaders, and it isn't surprising that we may be seeing the largest mass exodus from Christianity that our culture has ever experienced.

Who is to blame for all of this? We can debate that, of course. There is no doubt that the media, entertainment, and higher education industries can be highly effective in staining the reputation of Christians. As we will see, however, Jesus gave His followers the responsibility to manage the brand of Christianity. If we have a branding problem, it is our problem.

We are not experiencing the first occurrence of this problem though. Throughout history, Christians have faced significant branding and perception challenges. The early church faced a daunting task as it fought against the smear campaigns of the religious leaders in Israel and Roman leaders throughout the world. We can learn a lot from how Jesus and the apostles instructed the early Christ-followers to represent Christianity well. The early church's rapid expansion and the quick, thorough change in popular perception should be a huge encouragement to modern Christians as we face similar challenges today.

My fear is that we will continue the practice of many Christian leaders and adherents: choosing a counterproductive response. It's so natural to feel fearful and threatened when we feel challenged, and these feelings can lead us to create an "us vs. them" approach. Such an approach encourages us to take the stance of victims who are justified in using voices incompatible with Christianity. This response is not only in opposition to the New Testament's instructions, but it also adds more accelerant to the flight away from Christianity.

I understand why Christians are responding this way, however; that's why I decided to write this book. Christianity in America is at a significant inflection point. The next few years will either deepen the decline away from Christianity or spark a movement toward Jesus. Which of the two happens will largely depend on how Christians represent Jesus, and we need a major course correction. I am fully hopeful that if we embrace what Jesus taught, then we will win over a skeptical world that is hungry for what only He can provide. The emerging generation is not being repelled by Jesus but by a perversion of Jesus whom they see in us as His church. As we recapture our brand identity and mission—as a movement of radical love—we can once again be an irresistible force for good on this planet.

For those who have read this far, I wonder if you are fearful that, with words like *branding* and *rebranding*, I will advocate for changing the Christian message from one that is rooted in New Testament teaching or changing the core of who Jesus called us to be. I assure you that is not where this book is headed. The solution to the challenges facing the Christian brand does not involve being less of who Jesus called us to be, but rather much more. It is about recapturing an authentic brand experience that started with Jesus and was continued by the first Christians as they sought to win over an adversarial world through both message and action. The New Testament is a reliable guide, and our hope should be to restore New Testament Christianity, not obscure it. We will also learn from church history and marketing science. You nervous types can call that last one "general revelation." Fortunately, God gave us all brains—some more than others!

When you see various polls that show how quickly our culture (especially the emerging generations) is running away from Christianity, it may be easy to become despondent or defensive. This is what I call the "all is soon lost" mentality. We can give up and keep doing what we're doing, or we can see how God is working in new ways. Our culture may be turning away from the church and Christianity, but people still want what Jesus offers: hope, love, joy, peace, justice, transformation, and unity, to name a few. When Jesus and His disciples came across Samaria, the disciples saw it as a spiritually desolate place, but Jesus saw how God was at work: *"Wake up and look around. The fields are already ripe for harvest."*[1] God is always at work, and He invites us to join Him. He will give us the wisdom and stamina we need to reach a world of people He loves.

This book is most urgently about how we as Christians can recover the Jesus brand that gave birth to the Christian movement. We must admit that we don't simply have a perception problem; that

---

[1] John 4:35, NLT.

would be easy. We even more importantly have a product problem. This book is about how to restore the brand internally and how to better express it externally in culture, which involves living and telling a compelling story to a world that desperately needs to experience Jesus authentically.

Thankfully, I am not alone in guiding this conversation. I have one perspective as a "megachurch" pastor in Dallas (how scary is that!), who sees God repairing the reputation of Christianity in my own community. Joining me and providing their own perspectives are Mike Hogan and Dwight Jewson, two highly successful marketing and branding experts who work with some of the largest and best-known brands in modern, American culture. They are also close friends who come from two distinct faith positions: Mike is a committed Christian and a member of our church's Executive Team, and Dwight is a very thoughtful "none" when it comes to organized religion. They will inject general insights and provide numerous case studies from their work over the years with various brands that can serve as analogies to help us as Christians learn how to recover and better express our Jesus-given brand. I will let each of them speak for themselves about why they decided to help guide this conversation.

Mike

Much of my career has been spent building and growing some of the world's most powerful brands as a Brand Manager, Consulting Partner, and Chief Marketing Officer. I've worked with a wide array of companies—from Microsoft to Pepsi, from GameStop to Capital

One—in the US and around the world. I've seen amazing successes and huge failures. I've seen brands grow to become powerful, and I've seen brands lose trust and decline.

So, I guess it is only natural that I often see the world through the lens of branding. Just as a doctor will notice when people are sick and a car dealer will notice what people drive, I see brands and brand messages all around me, and I ask questions like, "What do they stand for?" and "How well are they keeping their promises?" As we will see in the next chapter, brands are everywhere, and the list includes many things that most people don't even think of as brands (such as non-profits, political parties, or even religions). All brands are attempting to stand for powerful ideas, and the extent to which their actions are consistent with the promises they make determines their success or decline.

As Jeff noted, I have been a Christian most of my adult life, and I have personally seen and felt the decline of the Christian brand over the past 30+ years in the US. I can't help comparing this to some of the other great brand declines that I've seen. This analogy—**Christianity as a brand**—is at the core of this book.

- Branding is about making and keeping promises about things that are important in people's lives.

- When brands keep their promises, trust deepens, and the brand grows. When brands get sidetracked and don't keep their promises, trust is broken and the brand declines.

- Christianity is perhaps the most powerful brand in the world, and it offers the biggest and best promise ever made (God's unconditional love and salvation).

- The church has lost focus on that promise and has become distracted with other things. For the most part, Christians have failed to demonstrate God's unconditional love and instead show anger, judgment, and selfishness.

The Christian church in the US is like a once-revered hotel or restaurant that has lost its way. It used to be a welcoming place where people would be respected and treated to an amazing experience, but the food has gone bad, the service is rude, and people no longer feel welcome. Just like the Pharisees in Jesus's day lost sight of God's purpose and instead focused on the wrong things, so has the church today (at least the most visible parts of the church).

The good news is that the same principles that apply to other brands also apply to the church. We will share stories of brands both getting it right and getting it wrong. We will share stories of brands that lost their way but were able to turn it around. Our hope is that Christians can learn from these stories and begin to refocus our efforts so that the church can become a place of unconditional love once again. We also hope to counter the voices of those who claim to represent the church but have only anger and divisiveness to share.

Dwight

I grew up in a large, urban, and liberal Methodist church in Minneapolis, Minnesota. In high school, I was the president of the church youth group and started college with the intent to become a minister. During my first semester, I was the only freshman in an upper-level class on the New Testament, and I loved it. I spent my junior year of college at the University of Durham in England, which had one of the most respected theological faculties in the world.

Then the church I grew up in decided to eliminate the role of Minister of Pastoral Care (which was held by a wonderful pastor and psychologist) so it would have adequate funds to celebrate its centennial, and it was moving in other directions that also felt incompatible with its larger mission. I was deeply disillusioned by what felt to me like a betrayal of the church's identity and message, so I resigned in protest. I've been what's called a "none" (not affiliated with a church) since then. (This does not, however, mean that I haven't had a strong spiritual core—one deeply influenced by the Christian church I grew up in.)

I noticed a discontinuity between the church's core values and its actions (and often words) that seemed incompatible with their core values (this is exactly what this book is all about). So, I changed focus and got a PhD in Psychology.

A key focus of my work has been on the identity of brands, institutions, and organizations as they seek to answer the questions, "Who are we? Why do we matter? What work do we take up on behalf of the society in which we live? How do we live in light of our brand and connect the dots between purpose and actions?" (Note that my theological training has always been central to how I think and practice.)

My clients have ranged from well-known restaurant companies to health care and hospital systems, from cancer treatment providers to financial service providers, from educational institutions and major non-profits to political organizations.

Mike has been both a client and a colleague over the last thirty years. In 2002, Mike asked me to meet Jeff and the other pastors of his church as a brand consultant. How might I help sharpen the ways in which Jeff's church communicated about itself?

I had very mixed feelings about whether to take the meeting. As a northerner who has only lived in blue states and blue cities and who grew up in a liberal church, I did not view Evangelical churches positively. I let Mike know that I had very strong theological and political beliefs that I thought would be incompatible with a conservative, Evangelical church in Dallas, Texas. I agreed to meet with the pastors, but I clarified that I had clear boundaries and would politely end the meeting if the conversation went places I was unwilling to go. I thought that would likely be the case.

However, I was pleasantly surprised. Jeff and the other pastors were genuinely interested in what I had to say. Yes, we did (and still do) have theological and political differences, but I felt heard and respected. I ended up meeting with them annually for the next six years.

In 2008, I was in Dallas for a business meeting and got a message from Mike asking me to have dinner with Jeff—just the two of us. I was curious. . . . What was this all about?

I met Jeff at a restaurant and knew something was up. There was a bottle of red wine on the table, and I'd never before met with Jeff alone. After initial pleasantries, Jeff got right to the point. He said, "We've been using our power on behalf of the powerful, not the powerless. That's not what Jesus had in mind, was it?" Jeff wanted to talk about what using the church's power on behalf of the powerless would look like.

I was stunned. Jeff's comment was not something I'd ever expected to hear from a southern, Evangelical pastor. This was a conversation in which I could wholeheartedly participate. Fourteen years later, we are still having those conversations, which have been a large part of the journey that led to this book.

I have a close friend who co-wrote a wonderful book called *Lost in Familiar Places*. Over the course of my career, I have worked with so many brands and organizations who became lost and disconnected from their core purpose. My work has been to help them rediscover their larger purpose and live in light of it.

That's what this book is all about.

Back to Jeff—Final Thoughts:

You are a big part of this, too—or, you can be. I'm sure it is why you have chosen this book. We hope to spark not only a conversation but also a movement of churches and Christians who reclaim the brand given to us by Jesus in a way that will prove to be irresistible to those we are called to reach.

01

BRANDS ARE ALL AROUND US

This is the chapter written by Mike Hogan,
who wrote the case studies with Dwight Jewson.

Is branding a good thing or a bad thing? When we speak of brands, many people think about slick marketers who are trying to sell us something we don't need. They think about advertising that tells an appealing story but is full of lies or half-truths. Maybe you think of the car dealer who says he must be crazy to sell cars at these ridiculously low prices or the OxiClean guy who screams at you. Unfortunately, these are real examples, but they don't represent what branding is truly about. The idea of branding is much bigger, and it's not just about selling.

Familiar brands are part of our cultural landscape, and each tells a story. The word *brand* refers not only to the name of a company or organization, but also to all the associations and emotions that the name elicits. Successful brands associate themselves with ideas and purposes that are important to their audience and extend beyond the benefits that their product or service provides. Here are some examples of companies along with my impressions of what each brand conveys:

- **Starbucks**: Offers a sophisticated coffee experience, but their deeper purpose (according to the mission statement noted on their website) is to "inspire and nurture the human spirit—one person, one cup, one neighborhood at a time."

- **Apple**: Sells phones and computers, but their deeper brand purpose is to provide user-friendly technology that empowers people to be creative and unlock their potential.

- **Nike**: Sells athletic shoes, but their deeper purpose is to help people perform their best and realize their unlimited potential. The famous tag line "Just Do It" is a compelling statement of their purpose.

- **Google**: Known primarily for their search engine, but their purpose is to organize and unlock all the world's information.

- **Heinz**: Sells ketchup as a comfort food that provides feelings of childhood nostalgia.

Companies spend millions of dollars to develop and support their brands, and for good reason. Research shows that strong brands outsell weaker ones. According to the consulting agency Interbrand, the world's most valuable brand is Apple, which is worth a staggering $482 billion![1]. Without question, branding matters for businesses.

Branding is about more than selling a product. Not every brand is a corporation with a trademark. Many things we don't typically think of as brands are in fact brands. Some of the most powerful

---

[1] "Best Global Brands 2022," Interbrand, https://interbrand.com/best-global-brands/apple/.

brands in the world do not sell products or services at all; rather, they represent ideas or causes.

- **Coca-Cola** is a brand, but so is the **The Salvation Army** (a non-profit organization).

- **Chevrolet** is a brand, but so is the state of **Hawaii** (a location and government jurisdiction).

- **Amazon** is a brand, but so is **#MeToo** (a social movement).

A brand is the sum of all the things we associate with its name—both positive and negative, both conscious and unconscious.

- **Positives:** When I talk about **Disney** or **Chick-fil-A,** most people think "fun" or "delicious."

- **Negatives**: If I talk about **Comcast** or **Monsanto,** you might think about poor customer service or genetically engineered food.

Different people might feel differently about the same brand, too.

- **Rivalries**: Think about rivalries like Coke versus Pepsi, Ford versus Chevy, or Ohio State versus Michigan. These brands are very polarizing, and the fans of one deride the other.

- **Personalities:** When Barack Obama left office in 2016, 45 percent of Americans saw him as "above average or outstanding," while 27 percent saw him as "below average or poor."[2]

---

[2] "Obama Leaves Office on High Note, But Public Has Mixed Views of Accomplishments," Pew Research Center, December 14, 2016, https://www.pewresearch.org/politics/2016/12/14/obama-leaves-office-on-high-note-but-public-has-mixed-views-of-accomplishments/.

Brand Versus Product: In this book, we will speak of both brands and products.

- In general, *brand* refers to the name and the idea/values being represented. The brand is the concept.

- *Product* refers to the physical product, service, or experience being provided. The product is the more tangible thing consumers get that (hopefully) delivers the ideas or values of the brand.

- For example, as noted above, Starbucks aims to nurture the human spirit (their *brand*), and they accomplish that through the action of providing coffee and a place to enjoy it (their *product*).

- A ***branding problem*** is typically a communication problem. A ***product problem*** occurs when the product or experience does not live up to the brand's promise. This is a critical distinction and one we will refer to throughout the book.

Brands are important for two reasons:

1. **In a highly complex world, brands help us to simplify and make decisions.** A brand is like a shortcut; it is a word or two that stands for much more. Imagine a world without brands. Daily decision making would become much more complex. For example, picture going to the grocery store, and with each visit, you must make a fresh decision about what kind of cereal, soap, or coffee to buy with no prior knowledge about what to expect from a given product. The brand helps us un-

derstand the product, but it can also evoke emotion. Maybe you feel better knowing that you trusted Pampers for your baby, Horizon Organic milk for your family, or Hallmark for your mom's birthday card. Brands help us make decisions, and their managers work hard to reassure us that we made the right choice.

2. **In a confusing world, brands help us define ourselves.** A favorite brand can be like a trusted friend who shares many of our values. We feel connections with brands that are committed to the same higher values as we are, such as pursuing equality, helping the poor, or telling the truth. Brands help us define ourselves within society because aligning with a highly visible entity that shares some of our values and aspirations is one way to communicate those values to others around us. We put brand logos on clothing, cars, and in dozens of other places because we want to be associated with what the brand stands for. Such a statement also tells others how we want to be perceived. Brands can be used as convenient shorthand for messaging about who we want to be.

- **If you volunteer for Greenpeace,** you are expressing your views on the environment and providing a point of connection for others who feel similarly.

- **If you volunteer for the National Rifle Association,** you are also making a value statement and are more likely to attract a different group of people.

- **If you order Grey Goose,** you are choosing a favorite vodka, but you might also be presenting yourself as a sophisticate who demands the very best.

- **What's on your T-shirt?** We don't just buy the brand. We want to tell others about our affinities and values.

  - A **Nintendo** shirt may tell others that you want to be seen as a gamer or a fun-loving person.
  - A **Habitat for Humanity** shirt might be a public signal about your concern for fair housing or the importance of volunteering.
  - A *Tidying Up with Marie Kondo* shirt might signal that you want to be seen as a minimalist or anti-materialist.

Brands are powerful because they link to people's core identities. Brand association isn't just about product quality. While it's true that brands can serve as assurance of quality or consistency, the brand message goes much deeper than that. It communicates intensely personal information about who we are and what we value. When we teach brand strategy classes, we often start by asking people to name a brand that they admire. Then we ask them to imagine that the brand became a person and walked through the door. What would that person be like? What would their values be? As they describe that person, we invariably hear something like, "This is actually what I'm striving for in life." The brand ultimately personifies some of their own aspirations. Who wouldn't want that on their T-shirt?

Some brand names have become commonplace words. The following are actual trademarks owned by companies:

- **Q-tips:** Owned by Johnson and Johnson. Other similar products are called cotton swabs.

- **Bubble Wrap:** Owned by Sealed Air Corporation.

- **Dumpster:** Yes, even Dumpster is a brand! The "Dempster Dumpster" was trademarked by the Dempster brothers in 1935.

Powerful brands can become part of our everyday language. They clearly express ideas that would be difficult to convey without the brand name.

- "Let me **Google** that."

- "We'll be drinking, so let's plan to **Uber** home."

- "Hey, you forgot to **Venmo** me that $10."

But what about branding beyond the corporate world?

Sports teams are brands. Think about the Dallas Cowboys or Manchester United Soccer—these are some of the world's most popular brands. They have incredibly strong fan bases and are worth billions of dollars. People feel deep connections to these brands and want to identify with them. We feel better when our team wins and sad when they lose. The team's performance affects our emotions, our self-esteem, and our decision making. An article in *The Atlantic* (Sept 7, 2016) cited a study from Louisiana State University showing that judges tended to give harsher sentences in the week following a loss by their alma mater. Sports branding is a huge business. According to *Forbes*, the Dallas Cowboys are the most valuable brand in all of sports and are valued at $8 billion. Manchester United Soccer is valued at $4.6 billion.[3]

Non-profits are brands. We don't typically think of non-profits as brands because, for the most part, they aren't "selling" anything; rather, they are giving something away. What comes to mind—both positive and negative—when you think of the following brands?

- **The Red Cross:** Do you think about disaster relief and medical care?

- **Habitat for Humanity:** Building homes for the poor?

- **PBS (Public Broadcasting Service):** Education and culture?

- **The Sierra Club:** Protecting natural resources?

- **The Gates Foundation:** Improving the world through projects like eradicating malaria?

- **Feed the Children:** Caring for the most vulnerable around the world?

- **Wikileaks:** Here's an interesting one. According to TopNon-Profits (a consulting firm that serves non-profit organizations), Wikileaks is the thirtieth most popular not-for-profit brand, as measured by visibility and web traffic.[4] Whether you feel positively or negatively about Wikileaks, there is no denying that it's a powerful brand.

---

[3] Ozanian, Mike. "The World's 50 Most Valuable Sports Teams 2022." Forbes. Forbes Magazine, November 8, 2022. https://www.forbes.com/sites/mikeozanian/2022/09/08/the-worlds-50-most-valuable-sports-teams-2022/?sh=4a6b7806385c.
[4] "Top 100 Nonprofits on the Web." Top Nonprofits by NXUnite, June 24, 2022. https://topnonprofits.com/top-100-nonprofit-organizations/.

People are brands. When considering how people are brands, we might naturally think about celebrities first, but it goes much further than that. Think about the brands of inventors (e.g., Elon Musk and Steve Jobs), world leaders (e.g., Joe Biden and Vladimir Putin), and athletes (e.g., Michael Jordan and Tom Brady). Even social movements can become brands, such as the widespread #MeToo movement. Even people who are famous for no particular reason can develop brands (think about all those reality television stars).

Countries are brands.

- What comes to mind when you think about **Sweden**? Happy people, friendly, egalitarian?

- How about **Russia**? Communist, Putin, political repression?

- **Bangladesh**? Poverty, starvation, violence?

Even religions are brands. What comes to mind when you think about:

- **Catholicism?**

- **Judaism?**

- **Islam?**

- **Evangelical Christianity?**

Brand perceptions color our thinking. Our perceptions of a brand greatly affect how we interpret other data as well.

- **The blind taste-test:** Food companies regularly have consumers test their products on both "blind" and "branded" bases. The blind test provides a product with no brand or package to indicate its manufacturer. The blind test measures consumer taste preferences, and it shows when they can't discern between two different brands based on taste alone.

- **The branded taste test:** This test simulates what happens in a store when the consumer sees each product in its package on the shelf. For strong brands, the branded preference is much greater than the blind preference, indicating that the brand name brings value well beyond the taste. During my days as Vice President of Marketing at Frito-Lay, we would expect Doritos to have a slight preference in a blind test when compared with other brands of chips, but in a branded test, we would expect them to win by at least two to one. In other words, the product needs to taste a little better than its competition, but branded packaging will be overwhelmingly preferred. Clearly something is going on here beyond just the taste.

- **A famous case study:** In 1985, The Coca-Cola Company determined via blind taste tests that its new soda formula was significantly preferred when compared to both Pepsi and the current formula of Coke. However, when they launched the new formula on the market, it bombed. They ultimately ended up reintroducing the old formula as Classic Coke. The company's most loyal customers were angry that they changed its one hundred-year-old "secret formula," seeing such a change as a breach of trust. The company learned that their brand is about much more than taste.

- **A brand halo:** Sometimes, perceptions about one aspect of a brand can give the whole brand a positive image, or "halo." Years ago, I was doing a brand consulting project for Microsoft, and we were working in India and China. We were interviewing small businesses and found that Microsoft had extremely positive brand perceptions—much greater than in the other countries we had visited. When we asked the people why their perceptions were so positive, they said things like, "The Gates Foundation is working to eliminate malaria." Their positive perceptions were about the Gates Foundation, but Bill Gates was so strongly associated with Microsoft that these feelings extended to his whole company.

- **Supporting a cause:** Your perception of a brand also deeply affects your willingness to volunteer or donate to a cause. Trust is critical. If you read an article saying that the CEO of a charity flew on a private jet and paid herself $1 million per year, are you more or less motivated to give money to that charity?

Keeping the promise: Branding is ultimately about making and keeping promises. Great brands make big promises about things that are deeply important to us. If the brand consistently keeps its promise, trust grows and so does the brand. If it doesn't keep its promise, the brand can quickly lose trust and decline. Brands fail over time for a variety of reasons; sometimes they fail to keep up with new technological changes (for example, railroads or department stores), but often the brand just loses focus on the core values that made it great at the start. When brands "break promises," people can be very unforgiving. There are many stories about once-powerful brands that have declined over time, leaving people to ask, "What happened?"

- **Losing relevance:** In the 1970s, **Sears** was known by the slogan "Where America Shops." They were, in fact, the number one retail chain in the US with over 3,500 stores. However, the brand slowly lost relevance as they were outflanked by Wal-Mart, Target, and online retailers. Today, there are only twenty-five Sears stores in the US, and the chain is in bankruptcy reorganization.

- **Failing to keep up with the times:** Much like Sears, **Blockbuster** dominated its category—the movie rental market—for years since its founding in 1985, but it failed to see technological change coming and did little to keep up. In September of 2000, Blockbuster's CEO, John Antioco, was offered the chance to buy Netflix for $50 million, and he declined. Today, Netflix is worth $128 billion, and Blockbuster is defunct.

- **Breach of trust:** In 2018, personal data from eighty-seven million **Facebook** users was illegally acquired and used without consent by the political analytics firm Cambridge Analytica. Facebook was ultimately slapped with a $5 billion fine for this infraction, and it lost the trust of millions of users. Even today, Facebook makes the list of the most hated companies in America.

People define the brand. Most of our beliefs about brands come from other people, not from the company itself. We might hear stories from friends about their brand experience (for example, how they were treated by an employee at a store). Others' experiences go a long way toward influencing our feelings (whether positive or negative) about a given brand.

- What if you went to a well-known hospital and found the employees to be indifferent and uncaring? Would you recommend that hospital to a friend?

- What if you went to a professional sporting event, but the fans were unruly and rude, and someone threw a beer at you? Would you go back?

- According to a 2018 survey by Gallup, only 27 percent of employees agree that the brand they represent consistently delivers on its promises to consumers.[5]

- Marketers use a tool called Net Promoter to measure brand loyalty. It asks only one question: Would you recommend this brand to a friend? The negatives are subtracted from the positives, and the result is a score that sums up the brand's performance. Of all metrics available to brand managers, this one—whether or not people recommend the brand—has perhaps become the most important.

---

[5] O'Boyle, Ed and Amy Adkins, "Companies Only Deliver on Their Brand Promises Half the Time," Gallup, May 4, 2015, https://www.gallup.com/workplace/236597/companies-deliver-brand-promises-half-time.aspx.

Strong brands make and keep promises. At the end of the day, good branding is about trust. Brands that break promises decline, but confession and authenticity can bring them back.

- Does this brand clearly stand for something?

- Do I agree with its values?

- Does it act in a way that is consistent with what it says, or is it saying one thing and doing another?

    - If a car company talks about quality, but its cars consistently break down, can I really trust it? Would I recommend it to a friend?

    - If a religion teaches love and grace, but its people are negative and bigoted, do I want to listen to its teachings?

Summary:

- Brands are all around us, and they are much more than just consumer products. They play a key role in how we make decisions and how we feel about ourselves.

- A powerful brand stands for something that is deeply important in people's lives, and it consistently behaves in a way that demonstrates commitment to those values. If the brand keeps its values, it grows; if it violates its values, it declines.

- The actions of people associated with a brand (e.g., employees, advocates, fans, and members) largely determine that brand's perception.

What key principles apply to the church?

- Christianity is a religion, but it is also a brand—arguably the most powerful brand in the world. Like all powerful brands, Christianity makes bold promises. Jesus defined the brand promise over 2,000 years ago. Christianity's promise is <u>God's unconditional love</u>. It is hard to think of a bigger or more powerful promise than that.

- In the US, the Christian brand is losing relevance and influence. A key reason is that Christians, who represent the brand to the world, fail to display the promises of Christianity. We do not consistently act in a way that reinforces God's unconditional love.

- To be clear, the issue we are speaking about is not people's rejection of God's message; rather, it is people's rejection of the church because they see that Christians' words and actions are inconsistent with God's message of love and forgiveness.

- When we speak of rebranding Christianity, we are not talking about a new advertising campaign, and we certainly aren't talking about changing the promise. We are calling Christians to live out the promise of God's unconditional love to a skeptical world every day. Christianity is like a brand that lost its way. We have forgotten what the brand is really about, and we need to regain our focus. In future chapters, we will give examples of other brands that lost their way and how some of them were able to recover.

02

THE JESUS BRAND

Every person reading this book is unique, but some people in our world stand out as highly unique in very specific ways. Their remarkable uniqueness becomes part of their brand. Take Albert Einstein as one example. We all know that he was a genius, but would he look as smart without his crazy hair? How about ZZ Top without their beards? Bono without his sunglasses? Spike Lee without his real glasses? Or Miley Cyrus without her outstretched tongue? These iconic people stick out because of their signature uniqueness that sets them apart from everyone else.

Jesus's teachings describe the characteristics that should make Christians stand out as unique. He invited Christians to participate in His divine mission by authentically living out the brand and attracting others to everything that Christ came to bring. It's interesting to note what Jesus did *not* choose as our differentiating characteristics. Our morality, frequency of worship, views on cultural issues, and ability to win arguments don't define us;

instead, our Jesus-given brand identifier can be boiled down to one very powerful word: love. L-O-V-E. It may sound sweet and even a little cliché, but the gravity of this word and the calling behind it contain great depth and significance. Jesus was not only saying that we should be kind and loving, but He was also saying something very radical that calls us to a completely different way of thinking and living—so different that before Jesus brought it, the world had never seen it. We throw the word *love* around so flippantly at times, but Jesus calls us to exhibit an extravagant love that is so far beyond the norm that it would be impossible without Jesus leading the way.

It's the kind of love that a watching world who finds our beliefs increasingly strange needs to see if they are going to take a second look at Jesus's claims. Just before Jesus went to the cross, He gathered with His disciples for a very significant conversation that took place during the Last Supper. This was the night He would be betrayed by Judas and arrested. This was the night He spoke His last words to the disciples before the crucifixion, and it was no doubt very tender and emotional. I'm sure you've had conversations with your loved ones that are so significant, you remember them forever. John, one of the disciples present, wrote about the Last Supper in his gospel, and you can tell that it was perhaps the most impactful evening of his life. He devoted four chapters in the Book of John to this one event, and he often referred back to these words of Jesus in the letters he wrote to churches many decades later. What Jesus said on that night marked John forever:

"Dear children, I will be with you only a little longer. And as I told the Jewish leaders, you will search for me, but you can't come where I am going."[1]

Jesus was going away, and His disciples wouldn't see Him for a while. He knew what was about to happen: He was going to His death on the cross, and He would be arrested in a matter of hours. So, these words are like His last words. As we all know from the movies, last words are important! Picture a scene in which someone utters their last words before their final breath, and everybody leans in to hear: "Tell my wife I love her," or "The treasure map is in the..." (and hopefully they get those final words out!). Similarly, when Jesus said these words, His disciples were surely leaning in to hear what He would say. And here is what He said:

"So now I am giving you a new commandment..."[2]

This new commandment would be like His final marching orders. The way Jesus words it in Greek (the original language of the New Testament) highlights the dramatic effect. The Greek word He uses for *new* is not the normal word for *new*. Instead, it means *novel*—a completely new, never-before-heard command. Jesus also changed the standard sentence order to emphasize the phrase "new command." Whatever this completely new command was, it was really big. So, every disciple was leaning in and couldn't wait to hear it:

"So now I am giving you a new commandment: Love each other. Just as I have loved you, you should love each other. Your love for

[1] John 13:33, NLT.
[2] John 13:34, NLT.

19

one another will prove to the world that you are my disciples."[3]

What? That's the big, new command? Love each other? That's it. The "new" thing wasn't even new. If Jesus had said, "Everybody get a tattoo," at least that would be new. Or even something like, "Wear #blessed T-shirts." Instead, He did this big buildup about a completely new command and then said, "Love each other." That had to be a buzz-kill! We know it was a letdown by the response: Peter simply ignored it and focused on what Jesus said about going somewhere they couldn't follow. It's like he said, "Oh, okay. Love each other. That's sweet, but what was that about you going somewhere?" Jesus spends the next couple of chapters dealing with the disciples' personal concerns, but then He comes back around to His big point, the new command, in Chapter 15. Unfortunately, the disciples were too preoccupied to understand just how new and significant this command was.

It might be easy for us to miss the newness of the command, too, because we all know that love is a good thing. What is so new about the command to love each other? The Old Testament commanded love of neighbor, and Jesus had already identified love as the essence of Old Testament law. Jesus had already given the Golden Rule ("treat other people the way you want to be treated"). He also already said that the command to love others even includes loving one's enemies. So, what was so new about the commandment to love each other?

The new part was what Jesus added after he said, "love each other." He said:

---

[3] John 13:34-35, NLT.

"Just as I have loved you, you should love each other."

That's the different part. He brought the command to a whole new level: love each other the same way Jesus loves us. Now *that's* next-level.

The disciples experienced Jesus's brand of love for three to four years during His earthly ministry. They were constantly amazed at His love, including just minutes before Jesus gave this command. At the very beginning of the Last Supper, Jesus—who they had come to believe was God in human flesh, their Creator, Sustainer, and Lord—bent down and started washing their feet. At that time, foot washing was a menial task that was only done by the lowliest of servants. Jesus humbled Himself and assumed the role of a servant to show love to His disciples. Then He told them to do the same for each other. He was not just referring to the occasional foot washing; rather, He was saying, "I want you to humble yourselves and sacrificially serve other people. Instead of making life about you, lift other people up."

Merely hours after the foot washing and the Last Supper, they would experience an even greater display of radical love: the sacrifice of Jesus's own life. As Jesus said in John 15:13, *"There is no greater love than to lay down one's life for one's friends."* In just a matter of hours, Jesus would give His life on the cross as a sacrificial substitution to take the penalty for sin that we deserve—to "pay our bill," so to speak. That's the love of Jesus—a new kind of crazy love that serves and sacrifices for the sake of others in ways that cause them to wonder, "Why are you doing that? That's way overboard."

In a world fractured into tribes and filled with hate, what's amazing is that Jesus gave his life for every single person in the world. In his radical love, he literally sacrificed his life to provide eternal life for you, me, and every person from every group, nation, and ethnicity. Christianity offers a wide-open invitation to every human being to find forgiveness and new life in Christ. This is all summed up in the famous verse John 3:16: *"For God so loved the world that he gave his one and only Son, that whoever believes in him shall not perish but have everlasting life."* In fact, Christianity is not an American religion or a Western religion. It is not a white religion or an upper-class religion. Following Jesus is for all people from all backgrounds in all places. As a matter of fact, Christianity may be struggling here but is thriving in more regions around the world than any other religion, making it the world's most culturally diverse religion.[4]

This sacrificial, arms-wide-open, Jesus-style love is what the Apostle Paul wrote about to the Philippian church to take on as their way of life:

> *Do nothing out of selfish ambition or vain conceit. Rather, in humility value others above yourselves, not looking to your own interests but each of you to the interests of the others. In your relationships with one another, have the same mindset as Christ Jesus: Who, being in very nature God, did not consider equality*

---

[4] According to a PEW study, "Christians are also geographically widespread—so far-flung, in fact, that no single continent or region can indisputably claim to be the center of global Christianity." As of 2011, 26% of all Christians live in Europe, 37% in the Americas, 24% in sub-Saharan Africa, and 13% in Asia and the Pacific. See "Global Christianity – A Report on the Size and Distribution of the World's Christian Population, Pew Research Center, December 19, 2011, http://www.pewforum.org/2011/12/19/global-christianity-exec/.

with God something to be used to His own advantage; rather, He made Himself nothing by taking the very nature of a servant, being made in human likeness. And being found in appearance as a man, He humbled himself by becoming obedient to death—even death on a cross![5]

Selfless love is a completely new ethic, a new way of life that says, "I am going to put aside my own preferences, pride, and comfort to serve others. I am going to be others-focused, not self-focused." This type of love even goes beyond the Golden Rule to "do unto others as you would have them do unto you." We are to love others the way Jesus loved people . . . and the way He loves us.

What is the anticipated result of all this? *"Your love for one another will prove to the world that you are my disciples."*[6] Love is our brand identifier, and it's the first thing people should think of when they hear the word *Christian.* They might say, "Boy, those Christians believe some crazy things, but their love for people is amazing. They are generous, sacrificial, gracious, and always kind. I may not buy into what they believe, but I would hate to live in this world without them." Sacrificial love produces an irresistible influence that draws people to Jesus, which is by design. Our legitimacy in a non-believing culture is not found in our beliefs, arguments, or morality; instead, it comes from our display of Jesus-level love. That's how the world will know that the claims of Jesus are true and that we follow the one true God who came to reconcile sinners to Himself.

---

[5] Philippians 2:3-8, NIV.
[6] John 13:35, NLT.

Radical love is the Jesus brand. It's the way Christians roll—or should roll. The earliest Christians embodied this love, and they turned their world upside down (as some opponents of Christianity in the book of Acts observed[7]). The Christians largely won over a skeptical world with the alluring force of the love they displayed. Church history demonstrates that the way early Christians loved people—including those who were persecuting them—was impossible to ignore.

Two thousand years later, we have the same brand with a significant problem: virtually nobody outside of Christianity associates Christians with radical love. We have a branding problem, and it is our problem to solve. We will dive deeply into this problem in the upcoming chapters, but before we leave this discussion about the brand of radical love, it is worth highlighting that the "new command" is exactly that: a command. Love is not optional for Christ followers. Jesus's invitation to us is not just, "Hey, come get a better life." His real invitation is, "Come, and let's change the world together." He invites us into a whole new lifestyle of crazy, Jesus-style, sacrificial love that involves us coming together as a church consumed with meeting the needs of those around us and welcoming everybody. He is always waiting to pour out the power of His Spirit onto a church that is all-in on that mission, and what God can do through a community that is living out radical love is beyond our wildest imagination.

---

[7] Acts 17:6

Case Study: Net Promoter Score—Great Brands Rise to the Top

We all have brands we like and others we dislike. Brands can be loved by one group and hated by another. Think about some famous brand rivalries:

- Ford versus Chevy
- Coke versus Pepsi
- Yankees versus Red Sox

It's natural for a brand to have a group of loyalists as well as a group that's against them. Brand loyalty is one way that brands help us define who we are (e.g., "I'm a Red Sox fan").

There are a few brands—though not many—that seem to be liked, or at least admired, by all. We may not be customers, but we can't help admiring the principles they stand for and the way they hold to them even in the face of pressure. For example:

- **Patagonia:** Founded in 1973, Patagonia sells high-end clothing for outdoor enthusiasts. They stand for a love of the outdoors and a deep respect for the environment. They care deeply about issues like sustainability, but they express that care in a positive, uplifting way (as opposed to the anger and spite seen from many other groups). We may not all be mountain climbers, but we can all support the idea behind the brand.

- **Starbucks:** Starbucks sells great coffee, but the brand stands for much more. The care and personalization that goes into every cup makes each customer feel valued. Starbucks is also known for popularizing the notion of the "third place"—not home, not work, but a place where you are welcome to stay and do whatever you need (relax, work, etc.). I personally don't drink coffee, but my wife and daughter are frequent Starbucks customers. I appreciate and envy the experience that Starbucks provides.

- **Tesla:** Tesla sells electric cars, which naturally are not affordable or desirable to all. But the brand pursues a technology-driven sustainable transportation, and that's a concept we can all get behind.

In the world of branding, one key measure of success is called the **Net Promoter Score**, which is a system devised by Fred Reichheld at Bain & CO in 2003 that measures a brand on a scale from -100 to 100. To determine the brand's score, customers are asked how likely they would be to recommend the brand to a friend on a scale of 0 ("absolutely not") to 10 ("definitely"). The "promoters"—people who gave the brand a rating of 9 or 10 and who love it so much they can't help talking about it—are added together. Then the "detractors"—people who gave the brand a rating between 0 and 6 and who are probably saying negative things about it—are subtracted.

(Side note: research has shown that people are much more likely to share a negative experience with others than a positive one. That's why ratings of 9-10 are promoters and ratings of 0-6 are detractors. Ratings of 7 and 8 are considered neutral.)

When the detractors are subtracted from the promoters, the result is a score that can be positive or negative (depending on which group is larger). You might think that a system like this would make it difficult to earn a high score, and you would be correct. In fact, anything greater than 0 is considered a decent score. Scores above 50 are considered outstanding. Here are a few examples of brand scores in 2022[8]:

- **Brands consumers love to love:**

  - Tesla: 96

  - Starbucks: 77

  - Patagonia 63

- **Brands consumers love to hate:**

  - United Airlines: -8

  - Facebook: -21

  - Bank of America: -24

---

[8] "Highest NPS Scores: Best NPS Scores from Top Companies in 2023." NPS Benchmarks. Accessed April 10, 2023. https://customergauge.com/benchmarks/blog/top-highest-nps-scores.

The key point here is that **the strongest brands are admired not only by their customers, but also by people who aren't customers.**

How do these principles apply to the church?

- **What are Christianity's core values?**

  - As noted in this chapter, the Christian brand's promise is **<u>God's unconditional love</u>**.

  - There are many things about the church that people may not like, but pretty much everyone admires unconditional love and acceptance.

  - In fact, research suggests that "nones" are most put-off by what they view as churchgoers' failure to reflect the love and acceptance of Jesus. ("Nones" are people with no religious preference or association; they have essentially rejected the church and organized religion.)

- **How do our actions bring these brand values to life?**

  - Brands like Patagonia connect their product to attractive experiences that help bring their brand values to life. For example, seeing people in Patagonia jackets climb Half Dome in Yosemite or kayak down the Colorado River can help us all love and appreciate the world's natural beauty, even when we aren't there.

- How can experiences with church people help others catch a glimpse of Jesus's perfect love and acceptance?

- **Do we live out these principles daily?**

  - The brand promise is only powerful if we are faithful to exemplify it. If a brand compromises its principles when circumstances get difficult, people will notice and ultimately think that the brand doesn't really care about their values.

  - Living out our principles is less about talk and more about action. What happens in a difficult or pressure-filled situation? Is the unconditional love still there, or does it take second place in the face of something else (such as a lifestyle or political issue)? Does the church really value unconditional love and acceptance? *Do our actions support the words of our brand promise?*

03

WE HAVE A BRANDING PROBLEM!

"Christians are full of shit!"

This wasn't a comment I expected to hear while speaking at a conference for pastors and church leaders, but it certainly got everybody's attention. I was speaking on the theme of this book—the need to recover the Christian brand and reshape the way people think about Christianity. After laying out the problem, a twenty-something girl raised her hand. She said, "I can tell you the real problem. Christians are full of shit!" When I asked her to elaborate, she was happy to oblige. She said:

> *My friend invited me to come today, and I have spent most of the day wondering why I'm here at a conference for pastors. I am not a Christian, and I have no desire to be one. But now maybe I know why I'm here: because I am the person you're talking about. I can tell you from experience that when I say, 'Christians are full of shit,' I mean that they say good things about how much they love people, but they are actually the biggest haters in the world. They*

are mean to people who are already mistreated. They are arrogant and pushy with their opinions about how the rest of the world should live. They don't even live by the standards that they judge everyone else by. If Christians wonder why people are turning away from the church, it's because Christians are collectively the worst of humanity. Some, like my friend next to me, are different from the norm. People like her keep me open enough to Jesus that I agreed to come today, but overall, Christians are the worst.

Her very bold and honest comment led to a great discussion. Thankfully, she left the session more open to Jesus than when she arrived because we listened to her and acknowledged her feelings, experiences, and opinions. She eloquently described the problem that American Christians must grapple with. Many Americans in her age group feel the same way; few outside of Christianity would connect us to the Jesus brand of radical love. This is the core reason why Christianity is currently experiencing such a large exodus: Christians are viewed as displaying characteristics that are the polar opposite of those associated with the brand created by Jesus Christ.

March of 2021 highlighted a major shift in American history. For the last eighty years, the Gallup organization has tracked the religious involvement of Americans. For the first time in history, less than half of Americans—47 percent—claimed to be involved in a faith community, whether it be a church, synagogue, or mosque[1]. This statistic had stayed consistently at 70 percent from 1937 (the year they began tracking) until 1999. After the turn of the century,

---

[1]Jones, Jeffrey, "U.S. Church Membership Falls Below Majority for First Time," Gallup, March 29, 2021, https://news.gallup.com/poll/341963/church-membership-falls-below-majority-first-time.aspx.

the nosedive began. Americans are still spiritual, but they are quickly turning away from traditional, institutional forms of religion.

There is a strong correlation between age and decline in engagement. The same study found that, in 2021, 66 percent of Builders (those born before 1946) claimed to be church members. The same was claimed by 58 percent of Boomers (those born between 1946 to 1964), 50 percent of Gen X (1965-1980), and only 36 percent of Millennials (1981-1996). While it is still too early to fully understand the next generation, Gen Z, there does seem to be a slightly further decline from the Millennial generation.

Compared to 2000, church involvement today is down about 10 percent with all age groups, and the largest exodus is among Millennials and Gen Z. The Gallup study's results mirror those of similar studies conducted by groups such as the Pew Research Center and the Barna Group. Researcher Joshua Crossman, founder of the Pinetops Foundation, suggests that 35 million youths raised in Christian families will no longer claim to be Christians by 2050[2]. Add to this the growing movement of Christians who are reconstructing their faith away from church.

I could bury you with polling data, but the results all confirm the same trend. The emerging generations are still spiritual, and many still claim Christianity as their primary faith identifier; however, they are exiting the institutional form of Christianity. To be more specific, the exodus from church is largely affecting white Evangelical Protestantism. The declines in Catholicism and non-Evangelical denominations were already happening decades ago.

---

[2] Joshua Crossman, *The Great Opportunity: The American Church in 2050* (Seattle, WA: Pinetops Foundation, 2018), 9.

Why are the emerging generations experiencing an accelerating repulsion toward Evangelical Christianity? There is a values clash, whether real or perceived, specifically related to the issues of diversity, inclusion (especially with respect to LGBTQ+), acceptance of others' identities, the environment, science, and so on. These are contrasted in the chart below based on the widespread self-perceptions as well as perceptions of institutional Christianity among these generations.[3]

Millennials and Gen Z	Evangelical Christianity
Open-Minded	Closed-Minded
Accepting LGBTQ+	Rejecting LGBTQ+
Intellectual and Pro-Science	Anti-Intellectual and Anti-Science
Inclusive and Kind	Exclusive and Mean
Diverse	Segregated
Fighters for Racial Justice	Perpetuators of Racial Injustice
Fighters for Social Justice	Protectors of the Status Quo
Protectors of the Environment	Climate Change Deniers
Spiritual	Religious and Institutional

The values that drive the emerging generations are at complete odds with the values they perceive in Evangelical Christianity. If you are an Evangelical Christian, it may be off-putting to read the stark

---

[3] "The Generation Gap in American Politics," Pew Research Center, March 1, 2018, https://www. pewresearch.org/politics/2018/03/01/4-race-immigration-same-sex-marriage-abortion-global-warming-gun-policy-marijuana-legalization/.

labels in the chart above. You probably don't identify at all with one or more of those perceptions. I understand, and that's probably why you care enough to read this book. In some cases, perception does align with reality, and in other cases, it doesn't. But now that we know how the emerging generations perceive Evangelicals, there's no wonder why they are repulsed.

If Christians don't change something internally to recover our brand and change our external perceptions, we will lose the next generations almost completely. In the 2000s, *Mean Girls* was a hit movie, but in today's world, Christians are seen as "mean girls," as bad, hate-filled people. It's astounding to think just how big the gap is between our intended brand image and how we are actually perceived.

The younger generations' decline in church engagement and their disdain of Christianity over the last two decades already had plenty of momentum, but the COVID-19 pandemic proved to be a momentous accelerator. We will discuss this more in the next chapter. For now, here's a case study to examine.

Case Study: Comcast—A Brand We Love to Hate

"We'll be there next Friday between noon and 6 PM." We've all heard those dreaded words. Here's what they really mean:

A. Your cable or internet is out, and the thing you rely on daily is not available.

B. A company that doesn't care about your situation will eventually get around to fixing it, but they expect you to wait all day for them to get there because they can't schedule appointments like other companies.

C. They may or may not actually show up within the given time frame.

In 2017, **Comcast** topped the list of most hated brands in America.[4] Reasons customers gave for hating the brand included:

• Billing for unauthorized services

• Difficult or impossible to cancel service

• Not showing up or cancelling appointments

The huge gap between the brand's promise to provide excellent technology and the reality of how people experience Comcast kills trust.

---

[4] Sauter, Michael B, "America's Most Hated Companies," 24/7 Wall St., January 10, 2017, https://247wallst.com/special-report/2017/01/10/americas-most-hated-companies-4/.

How bad is Comcast? We talked earlier about the Net Promoter Score (on a scale of -100 to 100) and gave examples of well-liked companies with high scores, even up to 96. The worst companies have scores below 0. Comcast's score has been in the negative for years. This means that for every customer with something positive to say about the brand, there are many more customers saying negative things.

Looking at this, it's tempting to believe that management at Comcast has meetings to find new ways to annoy their customers. Of course, we know that's not the case—I'm sure Comcast has plenty of competent managers who are trying to grow their business. However, despite their sincerity, they end up acting in ways that hurt the brand and undermine their core mission. **This is what makes them like the church.**

How can a brand lose its way so badly that it becomes one of the most hated brands in America? The short answer is **mission drift.** Most organizations have a good sense of their mission at the beginning, but over time, other concerns come into play that cause them to focus on peripheral things and lose sight of the reason they exist.

Let's go back to Comcast. It seems so simple: If Comcast provides their product (TV and Internet) consistently, at a fair price, and with great service, then people will love their brand and tell their friends. Then they will gain a ton of customers and make lots of money.

But as time goes on, things get complicated. The company faces financial pressure, and a misguided (albeit creative) executive says, "We have too many people cancelling service. If we make the cancellation process more difficult, then they'll give up, and we can keep billing them." To a desperate management team, this tactic might sound smart, but it completely violates their mission. Then the operations folks say, "We need longer customer service windows. We can't make specific appointment times because that's too hard." What's the problem here? Instead of asking how they could best serve their customers, they started asking how they could best serve themselves (even when it meant taking advantage of the customer). We've all seen this happen:

- Wells Fargo was fined $185 million for fraudulently opening credit card accounts for customers without approval.

- Facebook was fined $5 billion for selling customers' private data without their approval or knowledge.

- Volkswagen paid nearly $20 billion in fines and legal fees over its diesel emissions cheating scam.

How do these principles apply to the church? How is the church like Comcast?

Remember that we have a clear mission as given by Jesus: to bring Jesus's message of unconditional love to the world.

Unfortunately, we often lose focus on the love and grace of Jesus, instead focusing our energies on other things (politics, specific moral issues, etc.). Although it is entirely appropriate for Christians to have Kingdom-centered opinions and to engage in these issues, a problem arises when the watching world sees that we are so focused on these issues that our focus on the love and grace of Jesus is obscured. This is one reason why American Christianity is experiencing severe mission drift.

Never depart from the mission to pursue other goals. It's tempting to get drawn into other issues, but we can never let them overshadow our core commitment to the mission of Christ. When we do, non-believers are more likely to believe that we don't care about them. This reflects negatively on us, but more importantly, it reflects negatively on the Christian brand we represent, and it paints Jesus in a negative light.

04

THE COVID ACCELERATOR

The COVID-19 pandemic devastated the world in many ways: deaths, continued illness, shut-down businesses, financial hardships, damaged relationships, and the list goes on. Among the casualties was the public perception of Christianity in America. The pandemic should have been an opportunity for Christians to demonstrate the best of who we are called to be. While some Christians indeed did this well, unfortunately, the Christians who received the most attention were those who displayed the worst of the Evangelical movement. The COVID season confirmed many skeptics' worst suspicions, moving them from skeptical to repulsed. For many, American Christianity became a joke. It's a deep shame, too, because each of the crises that came together in the "perfect storm" were opportunities for Christians to demonstrate the Jesus way of unconditional love and grace. It has been said, "Never miss the opportunity a crisis presents." During the crises of the COVID years, American Christianity missed opportunity after opportunity. By "perfect storm," I mean

41

three major events that did great damage to the Christian brand because of how Christians responded.

The COVID-19 Pandemic

Over the course of church history, epidemics and pandemics have provided the opportunity for the church to shine through its display of love, compassion, and generosity. As a result, Christianity expanded rapidly. A vicious pandemic (possibly smallpox or influenza) hit the Roman Empire around AD 250, and scholars suggest that it reduced the population by as much as 30 percent. At the peak of the pandemic, 5,000 people died every day in Rome alone. As the pandemic raged, Christians—already a persecuted group—found themselves hit even harder as Romans blamed them for making the gods angry enough to inflict such a punishment upon humanity.

The Christians, however, quickly began to respond the way Jesus told them to—with radical love. Rodney Stark, Ramsey MacMullen, and other historians have documented the Christians' responses to this pandemic and others that followed in rapid succession. Such events quickly helped change the perception of Christians and their beliefs, allowing them to begin winning over a hostile world. The Romans and non-believers largely responded out of fear and desperation as they abandoned their sick loved ones to die, so as not to infect anyone else. Dionysius, bishop of Alexandria, wrote of the Roman response:

> *At the first onset of the disease, they pushed the sufferers away and fled from their dearest, throwing them into the roads before they were dead and treating unburied corpses as dirt, hoping*

thereby to avert the spread and contagion of the fatal disease; but do what they might, they found it difficult to escape.[1]

Dionysius went on to describe how the Christians in Alexandria responded quite differently, choosing to risk their lives to find the abandoned sick and extend care and hospitality even though many of them would get sick in the process. He wrote:

Most of our brother-Christians showed unbounded love and loyalty, never sparing themselves and thinking only of one another. Heedless of the danger, they took charge of the sick, attending to their every need and ministering to them in Christ, and with them departed this life serenely happy; for they were infected by others with the disease, drawing on themselves the sickness of their neighbours and cheerfully accepting their pains.[2]

This response by Christians was in stark contrast to the responses of others throughout the empire, and it also meant that most of those in their care—who would have died otherwise—were nursed back to health. Christian leaders, such as Cyprian of Carthage, also urged their people to love others who were persecuting them . . . *and they did.* As you might imagine, such a display of genuine love by Christians powerfully lifted the public perception of Christianity, and people converted en masse to Christianity during this pandemic and others to come.

Throughout successive generations and pandemics leading up to COVID, Christians by and large continued to practice heroic

---

[1] St. Dionysius' letter was printed by Eusebius in his seminal Church History, Chapter 7. The following English translation is by G.A. Williamson, published by Dorset Press in 1965 and again in 1984.
[2] Ibid.

compassion with similar effects. They valued the lives of others above their own. As a result, Christianity shined in ways that were impossible not to notice.

Unfortunately, the same did not happen during the COVID-19 pandemic. Certainly, many Christians did engage with others' needs in unprecedented ways, and there are inspiring stories of Christians who got it right and blessed their communities as a result. Those Christians, however, were not the ones making the biggest headlines; instead, to outsiders looking in, the Evangelical response to the pandemic seemed to be driven by anything but radical love.

Seemingly countless articles and news stories called out Evangelical Christians as the least likely to wear masks or get vaccinated.[3] And while most churches did choose to stop meeting in person as requested by government leaders, some chose to defy regulations as a protest to the government taking away religious freedom. If they wanted media attention, they certainly got what they wanted.

Please understand, I am not a virologist. I have no medical credibility to give a sound opinion about the efficacy of masks or vaccines, but I know that many people had serious questions about both. My wife, for example, is a former medical researcher with a biochemistry background, and she was concerned about the speed with which the vaccine was developed. I understand that some people had valid medical concerns and operated accordingly. That's not my main concern.

---

[3] "10 Facts About Americans and Coronavirus Vaccines," Pew Research Center, March 22, 2021, https://www.pewresearch.org/fact-tank/2021/03/23/10-facts-about-americans-and-coronavirus vaccines/ft_21-03-18_vaccinefacts/.

My concern was, and still is, the perception of Christianity. At the time, the primary reason for mask mandates, social distancing, and restrictions on large gatherings was to stop the spread of the virus and to protect the most vulnerable. Many Christians chose to prioritize their own views of what is healthy or effective above that greater collective call. In doing so, they gave the appearance that they were prioritizing their own freedom or even their own health above the lives of others. The few churches that protested by continuing to gather saw the government lockdowns and mask ordinances as violations of personal rights. I don't personally think that these Christians were in fact unloving, nor would they want to be seen that way. But many people interpreted these decisions as self-serving—the opposite of loving others. Unfortunately, the pandemic responses adopted by so many Evangelicals were picked up by the media and broadcast throughout our culture. These priority-based choices affected many outside of our faith.

I get the challenge, though, because I had to make these difficult decisions not only for myself but also my own church. My leadership team and I committed to making decisions about masks, social distancing, and gathering publicly with the principle of love in mind. Rather than asking ourselves, "How can we keep existing Christians happy?" we asked, "What decisions show the most love to the people God has called us to reach?" I wish that we had done this to an even greater extent, but thankfully, we took the opportunity to meet the needs of anxious people in a public way. For example, we raised money and partnered with our local YMCAs to offer free, first-rate childcare at our campuses to all essential workers in the Dallas area who needed it. We adopted hospitals to care for the practical needs of medical workers. Word got out in our community, and the pandemic grew the reputation of our church among the non-churched in our area in a very positive way. Not all church people were happy, however.

We were canceled by hundreds of our own members and hundreds more outside of our church; they thought we were either motivated by a progressive political agenda or had gone soft on protecting Christian freedoms.

I wonder how it would have been different if we in our own era had responded the same way that the early Christians responded as mentioned earlier. What if we had prioritized others above all other concerns, even at the risk of our own personal freedoms? Certainly, many did, but that was not what got the most attention. Instead, a golden opportunity to demonstrate an elevated expression of radical love to others was largely squandered.

Racial Tensions

When George Floyd was killed by policemen in Minneapolis, the racial tensions that had been building up throughout America erupted in volcanic fashion. The cell phone footage of the officer restricting Floyd's airflow while the victim said, "I can't breathe," went viral. Add to that the others who died during encounters with the police and citizens—including Michael Brown, Ahmaud Arbery, and Breonna Taylor—and the nation's attention was riveted by the cries of black Americans hoping to find justice in our society.

Most Americans in the emerging generations came alongside their black compatriots and similarly called for justice and change. One thing that unites members of the emerging generations is a deep passion for racial equality, justice, and reconciliation.

These events offered the church another significant opportunity because racial reconciliation and the pursuit of justice are biblical themes and mandates. For example, Paul wrote in Ephesians 2 that the gospel is about not only reconciling people to God, but also reconciling people to people, especially races of people who are at enmity with one another. At the cross, Jesus tore down the dividing wall between races, and this reconciliation will be complete in the new heaven and earth. For now, the church community should be a preview of that reconciliation and a force for unity in the world. Racial justice and reconciliation are *our* issues as Christians, and I would argue that the gospel of repentance and forgiveness, accompanied by God's power behind it, is the only force that can actually pull off the reconciliation that so many long for.

Though many churches did positively engage during that time of racial tension, most did not—a reality not missed by the younger generations of Americans. They perceived that the church was either indifferent to these issues or, worse yet, complicit. The church missed another opportunity to show God's love.

Also disturbing to those in the emerging generations is the apparent hypocrisy within the church concerning ethnic diversity. According to Lifeway Research, "85 percent of senior pastors of Protestant churches say every church should strive for racial diversity. However, only 13 percent of Protestant churches say they have more than one predominant racial or ethnic group in their congregation."[4] To preach ethnic diversity without taking the considerable effort to practice it is a hypocrisy that is too disillusioning for many to tolerate.

The 2020 Presidential Election

A highly polarizing presidential election in the middle of a stressful pandemic proved to be a key accelerator that motivated unchurched Americans to move away from Christianity—especially in the emerging generations. Most white Evangelicals supported the re-election of incumbent President Donald Trump,[5] and many prominent Evangelical leaders publicly voiced their support for him. While many in that number were able to separate their concerns about Trump's morality, civility, or humility from their greater concerns about policies, that nuance was largely lost on those outside the church. In some cases, prominent Evangelical voices dismissed Trump's character concerns as irrelevant. In essence, the media coverage suggested that the Evangelical church supported a political candidate in a way that deeply stained the Christian brand. Loaning our brand to any candidate or party (right or left) is always a mistake that will come with terrible consequences.

---

[4] Smietana, Bob, "Research: Racial Diversity at Church More Dream Than Reality," Lifeway Research, January 17, 2014, https://lifewayresearch.com/2014/01/17/research-racial-diversity-at-churchmore-dream-than-reality/.
[5] The AP VoteCast, conducted by The Associated Press and the University of Chicago, showed that 81% of white Evangelicals voted for Trump, and the Edison Research polls demonstrated a similar result of 76%. Newport, Frank, "Religious Group Voting and the 2020 Election," Gallup, November 13, 2020, https://news.gallup.com/opinion/polling-matters/324410/religious-group-voting-2020-election.aspx.

Lifeway Research found that churched millennials stumbled when influential Evangelical voices, dismissed concerns about Trump's sexual behavior and mistreatment of women while simultaneously preaching against sexual promiscuity. The double standard was confusing and often disillusioning. Jeff Brumley, a news writer for Baptist News Global, suggested, "Persistent reports that Trump had sex with porn actress Stormy Daniels is 'the last nail' for young people and the white conservative church. 'Evangelicals have lost all moral authority,' . . . And it will also lead to generational condemnation of American Christianity, which is complicit in oppression dating back to the founding of the nation. 'This current generation wants nothing to do with the hypocrisy of Christianity. We are rapidly approaching a post-U.S. Christian age.'"[6]

Regardless of our individual politics, when we attach our brand to a political party or candidate (left or right), our brand will become distorted. In the case of the 2020 US presidential election, Evangelicals who linked the Christian brand to a candidate who was viewed by emerging generations as arrogant, dishonest, and misogynistic colored the Christian brand accordingly. Evangelical Christianity became repulsive for many.

Summary: The trend away from the US Evangelical church was already in full swing, but the perfect storm of the COVID-19 pandemic, rising racial tensions, and a contentious presidential election greatly accelerated the trend. The outside culture perceived Chris-

---

[6] Brumley, Jeff Brumley, "Support for Trump could spell end of the evangelical church. But when?" Baptist News, March 19, 2018, https://baptistnews.com/article/support-for-trump-could-spell-end-of-the-evangelical-church-but-when/.

tians as out of touch, self-serving, and hypocritical. Skepticism turned into repulsion, significantly hastening the mass movement away from Christianity.

Case Study: Patagonia—Rising to the Occasion

This chapter spoke to key crises in our country, each of which should have been an opportunity for the church to rise up and contribute to the solutions to larger societal problems by demonstrating core biblical values of love, grace, and generosity. Unfortunately, in each of these cases, the church was largely *not* part of the solution. Instead, Christians chose to act selfishly and divisively, ultimately making the problem worse.

What about brands? How do they respond when similar opportunities come along? We've seen how brands might act to preserve their business in a crisis (economic downturn, product recall, etc.), but are there brands so committed to a higher purpose that they step up to solve a broader problem even when there is no clear, tangible benefit for them?

Popular brands are increasingly looking to link themselves to causes that their target market cares about. Research shows that consumers, particularly Millennials and Gen Z, prefer patronizing brands that demonstrate a commitment to a cause. For example, Starbucks maintains an ongoing commitment to fair trade by buying coffee beans at a higher price to ensure that the bean farmers can earn a reasonable income. Given the size of Starbucks's business, this practice is making a big difference in the lives of thousands.

Some brands take their commitments even farther. The

cause is not just something they support, but it is a core element of their business model. These are generally referred to as "purpose brands" or "cause brands." These brands commonly take the approach of giving one unit to a person in need for every unit sold. For example:

- Warby Parker: For every pair of eyeglasses sold, one is donated.

- TOMS: For every pair of shoes sold, one is donated.

- Bombas: For every pair of socks sold, one is donated.

This case study will tell the story of one particular cause—environmental preservation—and one brand—Patagonia—that seized an opportunity to make a positive difference. Patagonia has a long history of commitment to the environment, and its recent actions can only be described as going above and beyond the call of duty.

From its beginning, Patagonia has demonstrated a strong commitment to protecting the environment. Its founder, Yvon Choinard, started making rock climbing equipment in 1957, and in the 1970s, the company was incorporated as Patagonia. The company reflects Choinard's love of nature, and the products are designed to help others share that love. Their purpose is actualized in traditional ways, like donating a percentage of profits, but Patagonia has also formed more direct links between the cause to its business. For example:

- **Do no harm:** In 1972, Patagonia moved from using pitons (which scarred the rock face) to chocks (which are reusable and do not damage the rock).

- **Protect the environment:** 87 percent of Patagonia products are made with recyclable materials.

- **Protect people:** More than 80 percent of Patagonia's garment production (primarily sewing) is accomplished through a Fair-Trade program that guarantees living wages to workers.

Patagonia has always donated 10 percent of profits to environmental causes, but in recent years, that changed to 1 percent of sales, resulting in much more money being donated. The rationale is that the company would contribute to the cause even in years when it did not turn a net profit. This is a great example of a company elevating a cause above their own need to turn a profit. It's a strong statement of their commitment.

For these reasons, Patagonia is known as one of the world's most purpose-driven brands. In September of 2022, Patagonia's owners made a startling and unprecedented move that took their pursuit of purpose even further. *They gave away ownership of the company.* That's right. They donated 98 percent of Patagonia's ownership—a company with $1 billion in annual sales—to The Holdfast Collective, a non-profit that supports environmental causes. From now on, all profits will go specifically to organizations that support the environment.

For years, Patagonia's mission statement was: "Build the best product, cause no unnecessary harm, use business to inspire and implement solutions to the environmental crisis." It recently simplified this mission statement to: "Patagonia is in business to save our home planet."[7] Clearly, Patagonia is a brand that chose to step up.

How do these principles apply to the church?

- **Maintain focus. It is easy to get distracted and move away from the main purpose.**

  - In the corporate world, brands generally get distracted because the finance people push for profits over purpose. This emphasis might result in reduced product quality, excessive pricing, or low employee wages. Profits rise at first, but over time, the brand declines and people lose trust in it because the brand is not delivering on its promises to customers.

  - In my experience, churches tend to get distracted when a peripheral issue arises that people are extremely passionate about. For example, political

[7] Sonsev, Veronika, "Patagonia's Focus On Its Brand Purpose Is Great For Business," Forbes, November 27, 2019, https://www.forbes.com/sites/veronikasonsev/2019/11/27/patagonias-focus-on-its-brand-purpose-is-great-for-business/?sh=4bd7362954cb.

actions may seem compelling at the time, but in the long run, they tend to create division and undercut the church's core focus, which is <u>God's unconditional love.</u>

- **Make public commitments** so that you can be held accountable.

    - For example, when Patagonia stated that it would donate 1 percent of sales, the company publicly communicated its commitment and could be held accountable to that claim.

    - How can the church make similar statements regarding its commitment to <u>unconditional love</u>? Could it make a public statement regarding humanitarian causes, programs that specifically reach marginalized people, or something else? Surely there are creative and visible ways for churches to let people know how they share Jesus's love in practical and relevant ways.

05

CHRISTIANS BEHAVING BADLY

For many modern Evangelicals, the rapid changes in American culture (including the shift in perspective about Christianity) have created tremendous anxiety and confusion. A persecution complex is growing as Christians feel like the world is out to get them—to strip away religious freedoms and silence their voice.[1] They say that the solution is to "stand for truth" and be victorious when fighting with those who disagree. Many Christians think they need to battle in order to protect their freedoms and influence. In essence, they believe that they're in a culture war, but they're losing. With that line of thinking, Christians should assert their influence even more strongly so they can turn the tide and begin to win again.

If you buy into that "Christians as victims" narrative, it isn't hard to see why many Evangelicals are reacting so strongly. Unfair treatment

---

[1] See Michael Youssef, *Hope for This Present Crisis—The Persecution of the Modern-Day Church in America* (Lake Mary, FL: FrontLine, 2021) and Green, Emma, "White Evangelicals Believe They Face More Discrimination Than Muslims," The Atlantic, March 20, 2017, https://www.theatlantic.com/politics/archive/2017/03/perceptions-discrimination-muslims-christians/519135/.

of Christians may certainly be part of the story, but what if the current backlash against Christianity is one that Christians have mostly brought upon themselves? What if the whole idea of Christians entering into culture wars is a really bad, unbiblical idea? Unsurprisingly, when you fight against those who you are called to love, they don't appreciate it. When you make enemies out of those who you're supposed to reach, they won't feel the love.

We need to understand the massive mission drift and identity crisis of Evangelicals represented by Christian nationalism and its misuse of influence and power. The politicization of the Christian mission has brought about a misplaced identity and created the backlash that we feel today. Christian nationalism is at the core of the misguided and counterproductive attempts to regain influence. We shouldn't be surprised by the backlash because we created it.

Christian Nationalism and Culture Wars

Much has been written lately about the trap of Christian nationalism, and for many Evangelicals, it is an easy trap to fall into. Christian nationalism is the idea that America is a Christian nation that was founded by Christian Founding Fathers who based societal and governmental expectations on Christian principles and values; therefore, America is uniquely blessed by God with a unique, holy purpose in this world. If our nation allows these values to be eroded, God will remove His blessing. Therefore, Christians must do all we can to fight against those who seek to take our country away from us. Christian nationalism says that we must use our power and influence to establish legislation and get the right people elected or appointed.

"Take America back!" is a common mantra for Christian National- ists, which reflects an "us versus them" mentality and suggests that we should use our influence and the political process to restore America to its earlier status. Those who share this perspective will often reference Old Testament passages that speak about the nation of Israel, God's chosen people, as if America is God's chosen nation today. For exam- ple, you may hear some Christians use 2 Chronicles 7:14, which says:

"Then if my people who are called by my name will humble themselves and pray and seek my face and turn from their wick- ed ways, I will hear from heaven and will forgive their sins and restore their land" (NLT).

The idea is that if God's people (Americans) will humble them- selves and turn back to God, then we will once again know His blessing.

If this claim is true, how do we bring America back to the place of blessing? According to this way of thinking, it is our job to use political power to progress our point of view and oppose those who fight against our values. To help the process, many Christian organi- zations strive to use power accordingly, such as this example:

With strategic partnerships in Washington, D.C., it [the organi- zation] is able to be proactively involved in the effort to reclaim America for Christ. Whether delivering petitions; encouraging constituents to respond to critical legislation with letters, faxes, phone calls, and e-mail; fighting for qualified judicial nominees; or registering voters; the [name of the organization] aims to pro- vide a megaphone for the collective voice of Christ's Church.[2]

---

[2] Steve Monsa, *Healing for a Broken World* (Wheaton, IL: Crossway, 2008), 21.

What is the problem with this way of thinking? Christian nationalism is unbiblical and has led Evangelicals to misuse power in ways that make enemies out of those who we are called to love and reach. Let's start with the unbiblical part of the problem.

Is America a Christian Nation?

America is not a Christian nation now, and it never has been. This is not just my opinion; it's historical fact and good biblical theology. America is unique because many of its Founding Fathers were Christians, and many biblical values are included in the US Constitution (values which have certainly benefited this country). However, America is and always has been a kingdom of this world. It's part of the worldly system, not part of God's above-the-world kingdom. Any biblical principles that have been applied in America have been done so imperfectly and incompletely. This country is not ours to reclaim as Christians because we never had it to begin with.

John Piper states the biblical reality well:

I do not see America as a Christian nation. I do not see Christianity embodied in any nation or ethnic group. One of the glories of our faith is that there is no geographic center. There is no holy shrine. There is no national identity. We are aliens and exiles on the earth[,] out of step with every human authority and institution, even when we submit to them for Christ's sake. And we come from every race and all social strata and every nation.[3]

---

[3] Piper, John, "There Is Salvation in No One Else," Desiring God, January 20, 1991, https://www.desiringgod.org/messages/there-is-salvation-in-no-one-else.

Christians in other countries don't tend to view America like American Christian nationalists do. To them, identifying America as God's nation would be crazy. While they do acknowledge some great things about America, they also see the other side: our history of racism, our out-of-control materialism, our arrogance, and our tendency to use our power in questionable ways. In many ways, America is a wonderful country, and I am thankful to live here; however, it simply is not a Christian nation.

The Gospels recount a great conversation between Jesus and Pilate (the Roman governor of Judea) that took place after Jesus was arrested and before His crucifixion. The Jewish leaders justified their decision to crucify Jesus based on His claims that He was King of the Jews and that He came to establish a new kingdom, one that rivaled Rome. In John 18:33; 36-37, Pilate asked Jesus:

Are you the king of the Jews?" . . . Jesus said, "My kingdom does not belong to this world. If it did, my servants would fight so that I would not be handed over to the Jewish leaders. No, my kingdom is not an earthly one." Pilate said, "So you are a king." Jesus answered, "You are right to say that I am a king" (ERV).

When Jesus came to earth, he came as the King above all other Kings. He represented the kingdom of heaven—God's kingdom—rather than any earthly kingdom. So, when Pilate asks Jesus if He is king of the Jews, Jesus responds that His kingdom is not of this world; it's a kingdom greater than any on earth. Jesus was representing a heavenly kingdom to the kingdoms of this world, which really was a radical idea. His kingdom is the one that you and I as Christians belong to now. We are still citizens of earth, but our primary citizenship and allegiance is to Christ's kingdom, and we are called to do His work in this world. That's why Paul says in Philippians 3:20, *"But our citizenship is in heaven. And we eagerly await a Savior from there, the Lord Jesus Christ"* (NIV). We are citizens of heaven who are assigned here for a short time to represent Jesus Christ and to point others to His way of life.

2 Corinthians 5:20 adds, *"We are therefore Christ's ambassadors, as though God were making his appeal through us"* (NIV). We are ambassadors here, and we have a mission to represent Christ. 1 Peter 2:11 calls us aliens and strangers on this planet. We must always remember that we belong to heaven, not this world.

Christians are to represent Christ's kingdom on earth. We come from every culture, not just America, and our job is to represent the King of Kings and help people connect with their Creator so that their lives can be changed. Such a mission cannot be accomplished through power politics or even by spreading morality. As Christians, we are called to show Christ to a world that needs Him, and we must be a church made up of counter-cultural believers who model what God's kingdom is all about. That is our primary mission. If we remember this perspective, it will keep us out of the Christian nationalism ditch that has proven to be incredibly counterproductive. When Christians have fallen into that ditch, they have been pushed to the margins of the conversation, and it's their own fault. The church is here to represent Christ's kingdom and to say, *"The kingdom of God has come near. Repent and believe the good news!"*[4]

---

[4] Mark 1:15, NIV.

The Power Problem

Church history demonstrates what may be a surprising reality: Christianity is far healthier when it is pushed to the margins of culture, and it becomes very unhealthy when it remains at or near the center of power. The early church flourished as a persecuted minority. By the 300s AD, under Constantine's rule, it had gained so much influence that a once maligned and disdained religion became the Roman Empire's official religion. That sounds like something to celebrate until you learn how quickly Christianity became watered-down and corrupt. Countries in Europe would later incorporate Christianity into their governments, and you don't have to read a history book to see how that turned out. Just travel to Europe and observe the state of Christianity there. Christianity loses its essence when brought into the center of power.

Apply that thought to what we see in America today. My favorite TV show is *The Andy Griffith Show*, which takes place during a time when American life seemed simple and when Christianity was often just part of being an American. Many Christians would like to go back to such a time when God was part of daily American life. I understand that sentiment too.

However, the American Founding Fathers established our nation as a pluralistic society in which no religion would be established as the state religion. They had seen how damaging doing so had been in Europe, so they made freedom of religion a strong founding value to protect people from government-mandated religion. Such a structure was great for Christians for a very long time because we were in the majority. We had the power. But as culture became much more diverse and secular, pluralism lost its appeal to many.

The loss of majority influence and the resulting cultural changes have happened quickly. It's not surprising that Christians who subscribe to the nationalist point of view would be alarmed and fearful about the country's future. Remember what you learned about fear from high school biology? It has predictable psychological responses: fight or flight. When we're frightened, we will either stand against what we're afraid of or run in the opposite direction. Both of these responses derail Christians from pursuing our Jesus-given mission and representing our brand, and they repulse the culture we are called to reach.

One response to fear is flight, but when Christians flee from those who disagree, they make a mistake. Running isolates us and results in the formation of our own little Christian subculture that minimizes relationships with people outside of our belief system. We form a "bubble" with those who agree with us, and this contributes to the polarization found in an "us versus them" culture. Rather than engaging the wider world wherein we can build bridges of love and common understanding, we create our own Christian "ghettoes." Then we wonder why we are misunderstood and have so little influence.

The other response to fear is fight, which is the noisier option that would get the most attention from a culture moving away from a Christian worldview. It's what we saw during the storming of the Capitol on January 6, 2021: rioters with flags that said, "Jesus Saves" and "Jesus 2020" rushed to take over a government building. Perhaps some participants thought that they were doing the right thing by using power in an attempt to take the country back to what they believed was a much better place. That kind of thinking has been prominent among Evangelicals for decades. They engage in culture wars, using power to legislate, coerce, and silence those who disagree . . . and they equate these actions with the American spirit and the Christian faith. How could they *not* stand up for truth? The truth, however, is that culture warring has always been counterproductive to our real mission.

When we find ourselves relating to our culture through the lens of warfare, we lose sight of why we're here. Culture is not a battle-field; it's a mission field. There *is* a spiritual battle going on, but the people who disagree with us are not the enemy; rather, they are the ones who God has called us to reach. They are not the enemy in spiritual warfare; the devil is. Paul challenged us to relate to a non-believing culture in this way:

> *And the Lord's servant must not be quarrelsome but must be kind to everyone, able to teach, not resentful. Opponents must be gently instructed, in the hope that God will grant them repentance leading them to a knowledge of the truth, and that they will come to their senses and escape from the trap of the devil, who has taken them captive to do his will.*[5]

This passage makes it clear that some people are indeed doing the will of the devil, but that doesn't make them the enemy. Instead, they are held captive by the enemy. They should be recipients of grace and mercy, not anger and disrespect. When we fail to remember this, we often make enemies out of the people who God has called us to reach. Instead of seeing those who disagree with us as fellow citizens

---

[5] 2 Timothy 2:24-26, NIV.

who have different points of view (and who might even be able to teach us something), we see them as enemies who are out to destroy our country.

Twenty years ago, I took a group of interns to an urban ministry intensive in downtown San Francisco. While we were there, we served with an organization started by Elton John's foundation that prepared and delivered nutritious meals to those in the last stages of AIDS. Back then, the connection between AIDS and homosexuality was much greater than it is now, so most of the people we served were gay, and all were HIV positive. One day, I was chopping vegetables next to a very classy looking older lady. As I got to know her, I found out that she was a frequent volunteer, and her husband was chief of medicine at San Francisco General. Eventually, she asked what I did for a living. I told her that I was a pastor in the Dallas area and explained why we were there. I could tell that my response shocked her. She said, "Wow. I thought I had seen everything in my lifetime. But here I am chopping vegetables for people dying from AIDS next to a pastor from Texas." She stopped chopping, looked at me, and said, "I thought we were the enemy." I was so happy to look right back at her and say, "No, loving gay people and those afflicted with AIDS is something we have in common. We are friends, not enemies." That conversation marked me forever because it helped me realize how Christians can come across to others. We may have different views of sexuality and marriage, but we both love people and don't want them to suffer. As Gabe Lyons from Q Ideas often says, "The common good is our common ground."

A culture war mentality prevents partnership while damaging our real mission. Jesus never told us to create a Christian nation, impose our standards on non-believers, or try to preserve a particular culture. As I once heard Jim Burgen, pastor of Flatirons Church in the Denver area, say, "We think such activity is terrible when people like the Taliban do so, and we are not called to be the Christian Taliban." Instead, Jesus told us to help people develop relationships with Him, teach them to obey His commands, and create a new kind of community that demonstrates God's love and truth to the world. Instead of a warfare approach, He called us to take an endearment approach. He called us to stay true to biblical beliefs and to live in a godless culture in a compelling, contagious way. When we do have power, we need to act responsibly with it while realizing how dangerous misuse of it can be.

What if Christians truly understood what the Bible says about power—that God views it as a resource to be stewarded for the benefit of others? As Jesus modeled, and as the Old and New Testaments teach, God holds powerful nations and individuals accountable and gives power to some for the purpose of lifting up others. Imagine if we were known for the way we use our influence to serve others and lift up the powerless. Imagine further if Christians respected people who disagree with them and protected their rights to live out their values in the same way that we would like people to protect ours. If that's how Christians were known, people would be championing our rights rather than seeing us as the dangerous ones because we use our power to suppress those who disagree.

The apostle John reminds us that the radical love of the authentic Jesus brand will cast aside fear: "Perfect love expels all fear."[6] Love isn't afraid of people who disagree. Love doesn't put people down; it raises them up. Love listens. Love honors. Love refuses to see people as "the other" and then castigate them for being "the other." Love moves against the proliferating "us versus them" cultural mentality by seeing humanity as one group of people made up of individuals with innate dignity. Love finds common ground that allows us to form relationships with those who Jesus loves and calls us to love. This kind of love leads us toward the solution, which we will address in the next chapter.

---

[6] 1 John 4:18, NLT.

Case Study: Brands Behaving Badly—There Is a Lot at Stake

He overcame cancer in 1996. He went on to win the Tour de France in 1999 (the first of seven wins). In 2001, he was named one of the most admired athletes in the world. He launched The Livestrong Foundation and then, in partnership with Nike, the Livestrong brand. Millions of people wore the bright yellow bracelet as a sign of courage and determination.

Yes, I am talking about Lance Armstrong.

After all this monumental success; however, a confession came. In 2013, after more than fifteen years of cheating and lying about it, Armstrong finally admitted to cheating (doping). He was stripped of all seven Tour de France titles, and he received a lifetime ban from professional cycling. He lost his sponsorships and was sued for tens of millions by those he wronged.

Like some other athletes, Lance Armstrong fell from grace, but unlike most, his fall was directly related to what gained him notoriety in the first place (his sport) rather than unacceptable personal behavior. A friend of mine paid several thousand dollars for an Armstrong jersey back in 2000 and now uses it as a rag. Lance Armstrong is a prime example of how bad behaviors can quickly destroy even the strongest brands, but we could have easily picked others:

- **Facebook** was a respected and admired brand until the Cambridge Analytica scandal revealed that Facebook had been sharing the personal information of millions of users without their knowledge or permission. Facebook now regularly makes the list of most hated brands and carries a -30 Net Promoter Score.

- **Bill Cosby:** Once dubbed "America's Dad" based on his popular TV character Cliff Huxtable, Cosby's reputation took a 180-degree turn after numerous sexual assault allegations were made against him. He was convicted in 2018 and served time in prison. While his conviction was vacated, he continues to battle legal issues.

- **Arthur Anderson,** once among the most revered and trusted accounting firms, went bankrupt in 2002 because of its role in the Enron scandal.

Business and brands must earn their stripes every day. Think about a restaurant you used to love visiting before you started having bad experiences. Maybe the food changed. Maybe the service was poor. Maybe the business changed hands, and it wasn't managed well under new ownership. For whatever reason, it just wasn't the same. You probably came back a few times hoping for better results, but eventually you gave up. You likely told your friends about it, and they may have stopped going too. A breach of trust is the most serious infraction a brand can experience; it will lead to decline and sometimes even the death of the brand.

How do these principles apply to the church?

- **Any brand can fall from grace,** and it can happen surprisingly quickly when the brand's actions fail to live up to their promise. Even the strongest brands are only as good as the experience they deliver today.

- **Our actions, whether positive or negative, will strengthen or undermine our brand.** When we behave in a way that is unworthy of our brand, people will notice and tell others. There is always someone watching.

  - Consider Jesus and the church. Millions of Americans have been watching how Christians behave, and many have concluded that we simply don't care about Jesus's promise of <u>unconditional love</u> because we don't show it.

  - However, Jesus is still popular. In a recent poll, the majority of Americans reflected positive feelings about Jesus but negative feelings about Christians. They described Christians as "hypocritical" and "judgmental."[7]

- **Be mindful of the company we keep.** Think about brands that once associated themselves with Lance

---

[7] Paveley, Rebecca, "American Christians seen as 'hypocritical' and 'judgmental,' study suggests," Church Times, March 18, 2022, https://www.churchtimes.co.uk/articles/2022/18-march/news/world/american-christians-seen-as-hypocritical-and-judgemental-study-suggests.

Armstrong, Bill Cosby, OJ Simpson, and other fallen celebrities. Just as personalities can strengthen a brand on their way up, they can also damage a brand if they fall. Many pastors and churches were quick to support businessman Donald Trump when he seemed like a pragmatic outsider bringing change to the political process. But when Trump's lack of character became evident, they were put in the uncomfortable position of trying to defend the indefensible. Such hypocrisy was very evident to those outside the church.

06

TOWARD A SOLUTION

So far, our journey has focused on the problem, which may feel more than a little bleak. Our culture leaves people broken and exhausted, but these same people are longing for the unique and radical love that Jesus wants us to pour out. The church's current opportunity to recover our brand and win over a world that is "tired of the way things are" has never been greater in my lifetime. Jesus launched His redemptive mission to restore this broken world to the fullness He created us to experience, and He wants to use both individuals and the corporate church to bring reconciliation and redemption of all that is broken. Jesus's brand of love can only be found in Him, and it is available to everyone. Our world is as hungry as ever for real love that can only be found in one place.

That's where we—His church—come in. We need to spend time addressing the problem because our pursuit of a the solution can only start once we've owned the problem as our problem. If we see ourselves as victims of the media or unfair opponents of Christianity, and if we don't take responsibility to recover Jesus's brand and bring it to life, then we will get nowhere. As we've already discussed, Jesus didn't give us that option. He gave us the brand and told us that it would be how people know we're legit: if we love like he loved.[1] Again, if we have a brand problem (and we do), it's our problem.

Despite our current branding challenges, we can be confident that Jesus will empower us to do what He commanded us to do. We can join His mission and take our cues from the guidance He provided in the New Testament. Even though our current American problem seems daunting, it's nothing compared to the branding difficulty that the early church faced when Christianity began. If they turned their world upside down, then surely we can do the same.

One of history's greatest mysteries is how Christianity even survived its early branding challenges, not to mention how it became the most significant force for good on the planet. After Christ's resurrection, Christianity was comprised of about 120 adherents who believed in what many saw as one more "Messiah-wanna-be." In the Roman Empire, Christianity was perceived as a small sect of Judaism (a scorned and maligned religion) that seemed both ridiculous and dangerous. The Jewish leaders wanted Christianity to be stamped out, and they actively persecuted Jesus's followers. As Christianity began to grow, the Roman authorities also wanted it stamped out, and they dedicated much energy and power to accomplishing that goal.

In addition to constant, low-grade harassment and waves of severe persecution, the Roman propaganda machine was hard at work

---

[1] John 13:35

to define the Christian brand in a disparaging way. In *Destroyer of the Gods,* Larry Hurtado, recounts his thorough historical study of how early Christians were perceived and maligned in the first centuries of the church:

> *Christianity was considered, and really seems to have been, a dangerous development that challenged what were then accepted notions of religion, piety, identity, and behavior. Indeed, in that ancient Roman setting, Christianity was perceived by many as irreligious, impious, and unacceptable, a threat to social order.[2]*

Since Christians did not worship the Roman gods, they were seen as atheists who angered the gods and brought retribution on everyone else. Christians were depicted as cannibals because they practiced communion, a ritual in which bread and wine represent the body and blood of Jesus. Rumors were also spread that Christians were incestuous and practiced human sacrifice. Christians were widely characterized as "a class of people given to a new and wicked superstition."[3] Such perceptions gave rise to torture and persecution designed to destroy the Christian movement.

Despite the whole force of the Roman empire working against it, Christianity grew more rapidly in the first three centuries than any other religion in history, and it became the most dominant religion in Roman culture. In *The Rise of Christianity,* professor Rodney Stark calculated that in 40 AD, there were about 5,000 Christians (.0075

---

[2] Larry W. Hurtado, *Destroyer of the Gods: Early Christian Distinctiveness in the Roman World* (Waco, TX: Baylor University Press, 2016).
[3] This is a quote from Celsus found in AB Nock, *Conversion: The Old and the New in Religion from Alexander the Great to Augustine of Hippo* (Oxford University Press, 1933), 207. See also multiple examples cited by Hurtado in *Destroyer of the Gods*, including Tacitus, Pliny, and more.

percent of the Roman Empire)—an insignificant start. From there, however, he charted rapid growth until about 350 AD, when there were about 33 million Christians (56 percent of the empire). [4] In the face of significant challenges, the early Christians accomplished the historically unthinkable.

Some two thousand years later, the modern Christian church also has a branding challenge, but we can learn from their success. They accomplished then what we hope to do now, and history shows us that their effectiveness was no accident. They intentionally took responsibility to represent Jesus and live out His brand with integrity and sacrifice.

Jesus and the apostles who wrote the New Testament spoke often about our responsibilities as Christ's followers. The corporate church and individual Christians must love others and live in a way that authentically expresses Jesus's brand. Unlike Islam, Christianity's rapid growth did not come at the point of the sword. Instead, it came as Christians lived out Jesus's love through word and deed to win over a skeptical and sometimes hostile world. The world then was looking for the same thing it's looking for now—the very thing that Jesus came into this world to bring and that we have the privilege of living out.

Once we own the problem, we can work toward the solution. In this case, the solution is to authentically live out Jesus's brand in a way that people can see and experience. Jesus and the New Testament writers provided a guide for how to do just that, which we will focus on throughout the coming chapters. If we do what the New Testament

---

[4] Rodney Stark, *The Rise of Christianity* (Princeton, NJ: Princeton University Press, 1996).

instructs, what Jesus commanded, and what the Holy Spirit empowers us to do, we will no doubt win over a skeptical world once again. Our world is hungry for what only Jesus can bring, and we are the ones He wants to use to spread His love and message.

Case Study: Domino's Pizza—Ownership and Authenticity

Domino's Pizza was founded 1960 by Tom Monaghan. Since then, Domino's has revolutionized the pizza business with the promise of thirty-minute delivery and has grown to over 5,000 locations worldwide. The brand of Domino's is known and loved by millions.

However, as time passed, things changed. By the late 2000s, it was clear that Domino's had a big problem. The chain had established a reputation for fast and reliable delivery, but it was increasingly known for serving bad pizza. The issue got so bad that some customers famously complained that the pizza "tasted like the cardboard box it came in." In a national survey, Domino's ranked last in quality among major pizza brands (tied with Chuck E. Cheese). Unsurprisingly, the brand's reputation suffered.

Domino's own consumer research found that people liked the same pizza better when they thought it came from somewhere other than Domino's. Patrick Doyle, Domino's CEO at the time, explained: "We had somehow created a situation where people liked our pizza less if they knew it was from us."[5] Said another way, the Domino's brand had negative value. The pizza was worth less with the brand name attached than without it—surely this is a critical sign of death for any brand.

---

[5] "Domino's Atoned for Its Crimes Against Pizza and Built a $9 Billion Empire," BloombergBusinessweek, https://www.bloomberg.com/features/2017-dominos-pizza-empire/?leadSource=uverify%20wall.

At this point, most companies would make a few minor changes and relaunch the product as "new and improved!" They might launch an ad campaign touting their product as "better than ever!" But Domino's took a surprising approach to the problem and did something shocking.

- **They told the truth.** They offered radical honesty about the issue. Domino's actually ran TV advertising that showed consumers talking about how bad their pizza was. This went against traditional marketing wisdom, but it definitely got people's attention.

- **They focused on what really matters.** Domino's reworked their entire system from top to bottom to ensure that they would make and deliver better pizza. Note the focus on consumer and quality here. They understood that the bottom-line profit would only come if they made customers happy. Another important component of their effort was engaging the frontline employees who actually made the pizza. Domino's didn't just talk about better pizza; they started from scratch and actually made better pizza.

- **They gave it away.** They went out and gave the new pizza to former customers who had complained about the old product. Their message said, "We get it. We think we fixed it. Please try this new one and let us know how we did."

The results were amazing. From 2010 to 2020, Domino's sales more than doubled as the brand turned its reputation around and customers started coming back. They went from scoring last in quality among major brands to being ranked as one of the best. Domino's share price grew from around three dollars per share in late 2008 to over three hundred dollars per share today. During this time, Domino's stock even outperformed Google, Amazon, and Apple.

How do these principles apply to the church?

- **Don't bury the data. Be honest internally, and tell the truth regardless of how painful it is.**

  - The data clearly shows that the church has a branding problem. We must be honest with ourselves and admit that we have a problem.

- **Be honest with your constituents and admit to them when you have a problem. People will respect you for it.**

  - If your brand is disappointing people, everyone already knows it. You aren't fooling anyone with doublespeak or excuses.

  - They know about the problem—they are just waiting to see if you'll tell the truth or make excuses.

  - People will respect you for telling the truth. In

fact, they will probably be pleasantly surprised because most people don't tell the truth about their
failures.

- **Focus on what matters. Rethink your whole experience through the eyes of the people who you're trying to reach.**

  - Our branding problem didn't happen overnight,
    and it won't be solved immediately.

  - Step back and look at the experience your brand
    provides through the eyes of the people you want
    to reach. How are they likely to perceive it?

  - We need to ask tough questions like, "Are we lov-
    ing people like Jesus? Would they really associate
    our brand with unconditional love?"

  - Keep in mind that in the church world, our con-
    stituents include people who don't go to church.
    We are trying to reach them, and we must demon-
    strate unconditional love to them.

- **People are the key to the brand.**

  - Our people (Christians) must buy into the brand's
    vision and understand the reasons behind our mis-
    sion. Every Christian represents the Christian brand

experience every day. People will form opinions about our brand based on their experiences with our people. It's not about marketing, and it's not about media bias. It's about how people treat people.

07

A NEW KIND OF COMMUNITY

In order to win over a skeptical world by authentically representing Jesus's brand, we must understand Jesus's intention for the new community He invented called *the church*. As we will see, the church is a critical part of Jesus's core strategy to convince His beloved world that He is who He claims to be. This new community that emerged two thousand years ago during a polarized time in history is one of the key reasons why the Gospel spread so rapidly.

Shortly before going to the cross, Jesus spent time praying for His followers who would lead His movement after He ascended into heaven—this means that He prayed for you if you are a Jesus follower. You may not realize that Jesus prayed for you while he was on this earth, but He did. This prayer represents His dream for a new kind of community that we were all created to experience:

> *My prayer is not for them alone. I pray also for those who will believe in me through their message, that all of them may be*

one, Father, just as you are in me and I am in you. May they also
be in us so that the world may believe that you have sent me. I
have given them the glory that you gave me, that they may be
one as we are one— I in them and you in me—so that they may
be brought to complete unity. Then the world will know that you
sent me and have loved them even as you have loved me.[1]

Think about how high the stakes are in this prayer: "then the world will know." Jesus staked the veracity of His claim to be the Messiah on this prayer and revealed His strategy to draw people toward Himself. He prayed that we, His church, would "be one" and that we would "be brought to complete unity." The greatest defense for the veracity of Christianity should be our uncommon unity. We are a group of diverse people who would not otherwise come together, but because of our shared faith built on love, we form a whole new kind of community. Jesus was not talking about uniformity or a group formed by people who are all similar; there's nothing remarkable about that. What is remarkable is a diverse unity that is unexplainable apart from supernatural empowerment.

The world of two thousand years ago was arguably more stratified than it is today. Rich and poor did not mix. Citizen and non-citizen did not mix. Slave and free did not mix. No notion of equality existed between men and women. The racial divides of our day are slight compared to what existed then. For example, in Israel, there was a division between Jews and Gentiles (a word for all races other than Jews). The two groups hated each other. Jews saw themselves as God's chosen race

---

[1] John 17:20-23, NIV.

and looked down upon the Gentiles who were spiritually dirty and cut off from God. Gentiles considered the Jews to be out of touch, backwards, and arrogant people. Jesus came for both people groups and wanted to tear down those racial divides to form *one* new community.

Paul indicates that this was a central part of what Jesus came to do:

For Christ himself has brought peace to us. He united Jews and Gentiles into one people when, in his own body on the cross, he broke down the wall of hostility that separated us…He made peace between Jews and Gentiles by creating in himself one new people from the two groups. Together as one body, Christ reconciled both groups to God by means of his death on the cross, and our hostility toward each other was put to death.[2]

Jesus came to tear down the walls that divide us and to form one new community of diverse people who are united by what we have in common. Paul extends this further by saying that in the new community, *"there is neither Jew nor Gentile, neither slave nor free, nor is there male and female, for you are all one in Christ Jesus"* (Galatians 3:28, NIV). In Roman society two thousand years ago, this kind of community would likely have been deemed impossible, but regardless, this is the community that Jesus came to build, one in which the distinctions that divide us don't matter. In Christ, we are the same. The church became a community that the world had never seen, a place of radical acceptance and unity.

Just as Jesus prayed would happen, surprising unity began to be formed in the early church, and it caused people to see Jesus's

---

[2] Ephesians 2:14-16, NLT.

message as credible. The early church won over their skeptical world in part by forming a community that people longed for but had never experienced.

We have the same opportunity today. One day, Jesus's dream will be realized, as we see from John's description of heaven in Revelation 7: *"After this I looked, and there before me was a great multitude that no one could count, from every nation, tribe, people, and language, standing before the throne and before the Lamb."*[3] This future reality is God's ideal, and it's His design for the church to serve as a foreshadowing of it, like a preview for a coming attraction. If you've been to a movie lately, you know that if you show up for a 7:00 showing, the movie isn't actually going to start until 7:30 because of all the previews. Movie companies love to show previews because they are designed to make you want to see the upcoming movie. Similarly, the church is God's preview of heaven. We are called to be His community on earth that is so different and attractive that people know God must be real.

Now is the time to stretch ourselves, resist the comfortable pull of sameness, and intentionally form multiethnic and multigenerational communities who love and welcome "everybody always."[4] The world is tired of division and polarization, which means now is the perfect time to take up our calling and live out Jesus's mission. This is an important choice. Timothy Dalrymple, the CEO of Christianity Today, describes this choice well in his article describing the fractures within the Evangelical church:

---

[3] Revelation 7:9, NIV.
[4] Bob Goff, *Everybody Always: Becoming Love in a World. Full of Setbacks and Difficult People* (Nashville, TN: Nelson Books, 2018).

Rather than withdrawing into communities of common loath-
ing, the church should be offering a community of common love,
a sanctuary from the fragmentation and polarization, from
the loneliness and isolation of the present moment. The church
should model what it means to care for one another in spite of
our differences on social and political matters and affirm the
incomparably deeper rootedness of our identity in Christ.[5]

As we form such communities in this fractured world, we become positioned to help the wider community move toward reconciliation. Ultimately, the only real solution for racial divisions is the
Gospel of Jesus; it's part of why He came to earth. If people could
look at church and say, "Wow! Racial reconciliation is happening
there," then we would be able to make a wider impact. During the
period of heightened racial tensions following the deaths of Michael
Brown, Ahmaud Arbery, Breonna Taylor, and George Floyd, many
churches gathered together to set the tone of reconciliation and unity. The Gospel serves as a guide to move people beyond apathy or anger. In North Dallas, we helped gather together churches from every
ethnicity to form large gatherings of thousands at the courthouse followed by multiethnic small groups in which participants could share
their stories and develop relationships with people who didn't look
like them to foster deeper understanding and unity. Racial reconciliation is a prophetic and necessary pursuit for the church because it
is a core reason why Jesus started the church. However, the work of
reconciliation must be done within and among churches first.

---

[5] Dalrymple, Timothy, "The Splintering of the Evangelical Soul," Christianity Today, April 16, 2021,
https://www.christianitytoday.com/ct/2021/april-web-only/splintering-of-evangelical-soul.html.

Keep in mind that this process is neither quick nor easy. Once the early church began to express diversity and radical hospitality, it took years to come to life. The Jerusalem church resisted—so much so that, in the first ten years of church history, Christianity was almost exclusively Jewish. Much of the book of Acts talks about how God worked to break down the walls of racism and exclusivism. In fact, God waited to send the apostles on missionary journeys until the church at Antioch was formed under the leadership of Paul and Barnabas as the first multiethnic church. This was an eighteen-year delay! Yet, before churches could expand all over the world, God needed a church with the right DNA to replicate the vital parts of His design.

As was the case then, pursuit of a diverse community is still neither natural nor easy; it takes time and intention. As a pastor of a multiethnic church that is working to become increasingly so, I know that this work is difficult. Honestly, it would be so much easier to say, "Everybody is welcome, but a bunch of white people are going to make the real decisions." Of course, this would be terrible, but it would certainly be easier. Instead, we have developed a diverse leadership team that guides our church to reach an increasingly diversified community. We have seen the beauty in diversity as we attempt to build a church that resembles a mosaic of unity despite our differences. Churches who attempt to pursue diversity risk becoming too tired to keep going once they've started; however, the effort is more than worth it.

Imagine what would happen if we got this right. The world is frustrated with division and longs for real connection, so it's thirsty for a unified community. We were all created to experience connection, and the fullest expression can only be found in a community centered around Jesus. Imagine members of your community studying and experiencing local churches to figure out how we can do what nobody else seems able to do—and then finding out it's because of this person named Jesus. Imagine churches being at the forefront of present and future civil rights movements because our communities beg us to be involved and help lead the way forward. My guess is that Jesus was right (as is His habit, of course). People would believe that Jesus is who He claimed to be and did what He came to do. So, let's do the hard work, empowered by His Spirit, and work toward His dream of diverse unity.

Case Studies: Ritz-Carlton and Southwest Airlines—People Make the Difference

It is a generally accepted axiom among successful businesses that "the customer comes first." Innumerable consultants offer workshops and tips on how to ensure that a company does this well. Common tools that help companies put their customers first include:

- Engagement surveys

- Feedback loops

- Open-door policies

- Management transparency

Most businesses will claim that they do, in fact, put their customers first, and this approach is typically viewed as the best practice. But is it really the right approach?

Strangely enough, there are some very popular brands who disagree with the "customer first" mentality. These brands specifically make the point that customers are *not* first. And what may seem stranger, these are brands known for having outstanding customer satisfaction. It seems paradoxical, but it makes a lot of sense when put into practice.

Southwest Airlines is such a brand. Southwest publicly proclaims:

- Employees come first.

- Customers come second.

- Shareholders come third.

Southwest founder and former CEO Herb Kelleher put it like this: "Your employees come first. And if you treat your employees right, guess what? Your customers come back, and that makes your shareholders happy. Start with employees and the rest follows from that."[6] Over the years, Southwest has consistently ranked among the best in both employee and customer satisfaction, and it has delivered consistent profitability as well.

There is a concept called "service profit chain." It was coined in 1994 in a *Harvard Business Review* article by Professor James Heskett. Essentially, it makes the case that:

- Happy employees will be enthusiastic about the brand.

- They will deliver much better experiences to your customers.

- This results in happy customers who stay with your brand and spend more.

- The result is higher profitability for your company.

---

[6] Mutzabaugh, Ben, "Southwest's Herb Kelleher: Five innovations that shaped U.S. aviation," USA Today, January 4, 2019, https://www.usatoday.com/story/travel/flights/todayinthesky/2019/01/04/southwest-airlines-herb-kelleher-innovations-shaped-aviation/2483196002/.

Ritz-Carlton is a hotel brand known for the very best service. It consistently ranks at or near the top in terms of customer satisfaction, and it was named the top luxury hotel brand by J.D. Power and Associates in 2022.[7] Ritz-Carlton also sees the connection between employee satisfaction and customer satisfaction.

I love their motto, which is uplifting for both employees and customers: "We are ladies and gentlemen serving ladies and gentlemen."[8] Note the aspirational tone. This is a great motto because it elevates both those who work at the company and those they serve. Ritz-Carlton popularized the phrase "my pleasure" when speaking to guests. (Yes, Chick-Fil-A borrowed it from them!) This response succinctly communicates how the satisfied employee is motivated to help the customer.

While many brands spend millions of dollars to advertise the promise of great service, most of the promises are hollow because there is no operational or cultural effort to ensure that employees are in fact empowered and motivated to treat customers differently. In marketing, we say that this is like claiming to be "the friendliest bank in town," which is an empty promise with nothing to back it up. It's like when Buddy the Elf congratulates the New York City coffee shop when he reads their sign boasting "World's Best Coffee."

[7] "North America Hotel Guest Satisfaction Declines as Travel Volume, Room Rates Rise, J.D. Power Finds," J.D. Power, July 13, 2022, https://www.jdpower.com/business/press-releases/2022-north-america-hotel-guest-satisfaction-index-nagsi-study.
[8] "Gold Standards," The Ritz-Carlton, https://www.ritzcarlton.com/en/about/gold-standards.

It takes a lot of commitment to deliver an exceptional experience for both employees and customers. The proposition that employee satisfaction leads to customer satisfaction is not a gimmick. It cannot be forced or manipulated, and it requires truly caring for the employees and having a brand mission that inspires employees to strive for excellence in their work.

We see this same principle illustrated across many categories of business. A *Harvard Business Review* article put it like this:

> *There is a strong statistical link between employee well-being reported on Glassdoor and customer satisfaction among a large sample of some of the largest companies today. A happier workforce is clearly associated with companies' ability to deliver better customer satisfaction—particularly in industries with the closest contact between workers and customers, including retail, tourism, restaurants, health care, and financial services.*[9]

It's all connected. A business is composed primarily of people, and those people (as well as the degree to which they are genuinely committed to the brand's purpose) will determine the experiences your customers have and how they feel about your brand.

---

[9] Chamberlain, Andrew and Daniel Zhao, "The Key to Happy Customers? Happy Employees," Harvard Business Review, August 19, 2019, https://hbr.org/2019/08/the-key-to-happy-customers-happy-employees.

How do these principles apply to the church?

- **The church is composed of people, and its people will represent the brand.** What people in the church believe about Jesus's brand will directly impact how they act toward others. If they believe that Jesus and the church are threatened by the values and actions of those outside of the church, they will display anger and hostility to the culture at large. On the other hand, if they believe in love, grace, and mercy, then those characteristics will shine through.

- **Actions are far more powerful than words.** Christians—the representatives of Jesus's brand—must not only preach the truth of God's love, but they must also live it out. Our brand will only be as strong as our actions.

08

ATTRACTIVE LIVES

The role of "brand ambassador" seems to belong in the category of jobs that didn't exist when I was growing up—alongside video game designer, Uber driver, and social media influencer. But the truth is, such a role dates at least back to the days of early Christianity, and all Jesus followers have been given the job whether we realize it or not!

As a teenager, I was significantly impacted while reading the memoir of Sheldon Vanauken, a former atheist who came to know Jesus while in contact with professor C.S. Lewis and other Christians at the University of Oxford. In a journal entry from the early days of his spiritual journey, he wrote: "*The best argument for Christianity is Christians: their joy, their certainty, their completeness. But the strongest argument against Christianity is also Christians—when they are sombre and joyless, when they are self-righteous and smug in complacent consecration, when they are narrow and repressive, then Christianity dies a thousand deaths.*"[1] As a new believer with mostly non-believing

---

[1] Sheldon Vanauken, *A Severe Mercy* (New York: HarperCollins, 1977).

friends in my high school, I realized that it was my job to represent Jesus well because people's experiences with me could impact how open they were to Christianity. Once I became serious about my faith, one of the first things I did was find a way to discover other Christians in my school. With one Christian friend I already knew, I started an organization called Fellowship of Christian Students. The whole point was to gather together and encourage one another to live and love in ways that would make Christianity attractive to our lost friends. It was worth doing because that's how I met my wife! It was also worth doing because we saw many people begin a relationship with Jesus because they were invited to do so by people they respected.

I would bet that part of your conversion story includes a relationship with someone who was different in an attractive way. Something about them pulled you toward whatever they had discovered. They were a brand ambassador who attracted you to Jesus.

The apostles made sure that Christians would understand the important responsibility to represent Jesus to those outside the faith. The Christians to whom they wrote were misunderstood and slandered. Such treatment was unfair, and they had good enough reason to respond with anger or try to fight back somehow. However, the apostles were clear that a better way to win over their skeptical and hostile world was to live in a manner so attractive that a life of following Jesus would be irresistible. As Jesus was changing the lives of Christians to become more like Him, they were to display the fruit of His work in their lives in a way that was compelling and contagious.

The New Testament provides many commands related to living like Christ, and it is worthwhile to do a quick but exhaustive survey. No Christian should have any doubt about the vital responsibility as believers to represent Jesus well through the way we live among non-believers. Below is an overview of these commands. Let me encourage you to read through all of them and recognize the significance of YOUR responsibility. You (yes, YOU!) are called by Jesus and placed right where you are to be His brand ambassador to people He supremely loves. Here we go:

1 Thessalonians 4:9-12 (NIV): "Now about your love for one another we do not need to write to you, for you yourselves have been taught by God to love each other. And in fact, you do love all of God's family throughout Macedonia. Yet we urge you, brothers and sisters, to do so more and more, and to make it your ambition to lead a quiet life: You should mind your own business and work with your hands, just as we told you, so that your daily life may win the respect of outsiders and so that you will not be dependent on anybody."

1 Peter 2:9, 11-12 (NLT): "But you are not like that, for you are a chosen people. You are royal priests, a holy nation, God's very own possession. As a result, you can show others the goodness of God, for he called you out of the darkness into his wonderful light. Dear friends, I warn you as 'temporary residents and foreigners' to keep away from worldly desires that wage war against your very souls. Be careful to live properly among your unbelieving neighbors. Then even if they accuse you of doing wrong, they will see your honorable behavior, and they will give honor to God when he judges the world."

1 Peter 2:15-17 (NLT): "It is God's will that your honorable lives should silence those ignorant people who make foolish accusations against you. For you are free, yet you are God's slaves, so don't use your freedom as an excuse to do evil. Respect everyone and love the family of believers. Fear God and respect the king."

1 Peter 3:13-16 (NLT): "Now, who will want to harm you if you are eager to do good? But even if you suffer for doing what is right, God will reward you for it. So don't worry or be afraid of their threats. Instead, you must worship Christ as Lord of your life. And if someone asks about your hope as a believer, always be ready to explain it. But do this in a gentle and respectful way. Keep your conscience clear. Then if people speak against you, they will be ashamed when they see what a good life you live because you belong to Christ."

Colossians 4:5-6 (NLT): "Live wisely among those who are not believers, and make the most of every opportunity. Let your conversation be gracious and attractive so that you will have the right response for everyone."

1 Timothy 3:6-7 (NLT): "A church leader must not be a new believer, because he might become proud, and the devil would cause him to fall. Also, people outside the church must speak well of him so that he will not be disgraced and fall into the devil's trap."

Philippians 2:14-15 (NLT): "Do everything without complaining and arguing, so that no one can criticize you. Live clean, innocent lives as children of God, shining like bright lights in a world full of crooked and perverse people."

Titus 2:3-14 (NLT): "Similarly, teach the older women to live in a way that honors God. They must not slander others or be heavy drinkers. Instead, they should teach others what is good. These older women must train the younger women to love their husbands and their children, to live wisely and be pure, to work in their homes, to do good, and to be submissive to their husbands. Then they will not bring shame on the word of God.

"In the same way, encourage the young men to live wisely. And you yourself must be an example to them by doing good works of every kind. Let everything you do reflect the integrity and seriousness of your teaching. Teach the truth so that your teaching can't be criticized. Then those who oppose us will be ashamed and have nothing bad to say about us.

"Slaves must always obey their masters and do their best to please them. They must not talk back or steal, but must show themselves to be entirely trustworthy and good. Then they will make the teaching about God our Savior attractive in every way.

"For the grace of God has been revealed, bringing salvation to all people. And we are instructed to turn from godless living and sinful pleasures. We should live in this evil world with wisdom, righteousness, and devotion to God, while we look forward with hope to that wonderful day when the glory of our great God and Savior, Jesus Christ, will be revealed. He gave his life to free us from every kind of sin, to cleanse us, and to make us his very own people, totally committed to doing good deeds."

2 Corinthians 5:20 (NIV): "We are therefore Christ's ambassadors, as though God were making his appeal through us. We implore you on Christ's behalf: Be reconciled to God."

Do you get the idea? We are Christ's brand ambassadors! These passages remind us to be careful and intentional with the way we live in culture because we represent Christ. People's experiences with us will influence how they perceive Christianity.

When we feel unfairly rejected, it may seem easier to focus on the behavior of those outside the faith rather than our own. We could focus on the atrocious behavior of a culture spinning away from Christian values, but instead, Paul indicated that our attention should be focused on the behavior of believers:

I wrote to you in my letter not to associate with sexually immoral people—not at all meaning the people of this world who are immoral, or the greedy and swindlers, or idolaters. In that case you would have to leave this world. But now I am writing to you that you must not associate with anyone who claims to be a brother or sister but is sexually immoral or greedy, an idolater or slanderer, a drunkard or swindler. Do not even eat with such people. What business is it of mine to judge those outside the church? Are you not to judge those inside?[2]

We should hold ourselves and our fellow believers accountable to the standards we signed up for, but how can we possibly expect those outside the faith to live as if they had signed up too? As we read above, Christians are to "mind our own business" while living as His faithful followers rather than meddling in the lives of those who don't know Jesus. Why would we? Without the empowering presence of the Holy Spirit, no one can live how we are called to live. Our job isn't to convince non-believers to act better; instead, we are called to draw them into a relationship with Jesus (and improved behavior would be the natural outflow). After all, only He can truly change hearts and lives!

Mike Hogan, one of my co-authors in this book, serves as a volunteer member of our church's executive team. His life has impacted me in many ways. I'll always remember one observation he made years ago about how Jesus influenced others: not by push, but by pull. He lived, loved, and taught in a way that attracted people to Him. He created suction and curiosity—He created pull. When Christians

---

[2] 1 Corinthians 5:9-12, NIV.

get pushy, outsiders will naturally be repelled. We are called to get "pully," to live winsome and attractive lives. Jesus referred to this as being "salt," an attractive additive that creates an appetite for more, not less.

Here are some challenging questions to ask ourselves:

- Am I careful and intentional with how I behave among outsiders in my everyday life?

- Do I consider every placement as an assignment from God to reach people around me whom He desperately loves?

- Are people being pulled closer to Jesus because of the way I live and relate to them?

- How would the outsiders in my life describe Christians based on what they see in me?

If we hope to win over our world, we must realize our responsibility. If we take this responsibility seriously, then people will become curious and want to know why we live this way. We should be ready to explain the reason for the hope that we have.[3] People in our culture are hungry for what only Jesus can offer, and we are His brand ambassadors with the responsibility to help them connect to Him.

---

[3] See 1 Peter 3:15, NLT.

Case Study: Bumble—Creating Brand Ambassadors

As previously discussed, Christians are the brand ambassadors of Christ, tasked with the responsibility of bringing His message to the world around us. Those outside the church are watching us (our actions much more than our words) and drawing conclusions about the brand:

- Does the brand seem authentic?

- Does it offer something that I find worthwhile?

- Do the people behind the brand truly care about me, or are they just looking out for their own interests?

In the branding world, the same is true: people look to the brand's representatives and draw conclusions accordingly. Because of this, the role of brand ambassador can be a very lucrative one. Consider the following:

- Christian Dior has paid Charlize Theron over $55 million to represent their brand.

- UNIQLO paid Roger Federer $300 million to represent them instead of Nike.

- Nike paid Christiano Ronaldo $1 billion (yes, *billion*) to represent their brand.

Clearly, brands see great value in such relationships to pay their ambassadors so richly. But it also works the other way around. I found the following story both enlightening and humorous: Abercrombie & Fitch offered to pay a cast member of the reality show *Jersey Shore* to *stop* wearing their clothes! As a brand spokesperson explained, "We are deeply concerned that Mr. Sorrentino's association with our brand could cause significant damage to our image. We have therefore offered a substantial payment to Michael 'The Situation' Sorrentino and the producers of MTV's *Jersey Shore* to have the character wear an alternate brand. We have also extended this offer to other members of the cast, and are urgently [a]waiting a response."[4]

While big brands often pay extravagant amounts of money to celebrities, other brands prefer to enroll everyday brand users as representatives. These are everyday people who believe strongly in the brand's purpose and devote their time to living it out. One such brand that was literally built on ambassador deals is Bumble.

Bumble was able to penetrate the crowded dating app space and carve out a significant market share in only a few years. What makes Bumble unique? The answer to this question begins with their mission statement: *"Bumble is a platform and community that creates empowering connections in love, life, and work. We promote accountability, equality,*

---

[4] Sweney, Mark, "Jersey Shore's The Situation offered cash not to wear Abercrombie and Fitch," The Guardian, August 17, 2011, https://www.theguardian.com/media/2011/aug/17/jersey-shore-situation-abercrombie-fitch.

and kindness in an effort to end misogyny and re-write archaic gender roles. . . ." This in turn drives their unique operating model: *". . . On Bumble, women always make the first move."*[5]

Bumble ambassadors are typically college-aged females who are invited to represent the brand. It is worth noting that they are not invited to "promote Bumble" but rather to *"foster a world free of misogyny where all relationships are equitable, healthy, and safe."*[6] This is a higher-order mission! The passion and devotion of these ambassadors has enabled Bumble to become the third-largest dating app in the world with over 42 million monthly users.

How do these principles apply to the church?

- **Christianity is a people-driven brand:** As a people-driven brand with strong core values, **we will ultimately be judged by how our "brand ambassadors" behave around others.**

- **We have an amazing mission, and we always need to be calling people to a higher purpose.** Brands like Bumble certainly call their customers to a higher purpose. But how much greater is the church's mission? Getting sidetracked on anything less than exhibiting Jesus's love and grace would be a massive failure for the brand.

[5] "About Bumble," JobSage, https://www.jobsage.com/companies/about/bumble.
[6] "Life As a Bumble Honey," Bumble, https://thebeehive.bumble.com/ambassadors-bumble-honey.

- **Recruiting ambassadors is necessary to our mission.** Many churches are run like clubs: for the benefit and convenience of the most regular members or attenders. But what if we turned that around? The church's role is not just to attract the same people again and again, but to equip them to go out and reach others, to encourage them to embody the values of Jesus's brand and act as representatives. A brand like Bumble actively recruits and compensates people to do this. The church may not pay its brand ambassadors, but we should at least help Christians develop the mindset of a brand representative.

- **Someone is always watching.** How would Christians behave differently if we believed that every move we make could be seen by a non-Christian and affect their view of Christ?

  - Would we drive differently?

  - Would we talk differently?

  - Would we be more likely to stop and care?

09

DOING GOOD

There are some great advertising slogans out there and, of course, many awful ones! It may be hard to believe, but these bad slogans were actually used:

- Electrolux Vacuums: Nothing Sucks Like Electrolux!

- Uzbekistan Airways: Good Luck!

- Hot Pockets: Every Bite Is a Different Temperature!

One of my favorite slogans belongs to the Salvation Army: *Doing the Most Good*. Their slogan is a good one because it defines their mission and reflects their standing as an organization known for low overhead and a high percentage of donations actually going to the people served. The slogan also reflects a deeply biblical command applicable to all of Jesus's followers.

In the Sermon on the Mount, a powerful sermon that laid out His new way of life for His followers, Jesus further fleshed out the calling of Christians to live out the faith in a way that would attract those on the outside. In the sermon, He gave this command:

You are the light of the world. A town built on a hill cannot be hidden. Neither do people light a lamp and put it under a bowl. Instead they put it on its stand, and it gives light to everyone in the house. In the same way, let your light shine before others, that they may see your good deeds and glorify your Father in heaven.[1]

As Christ's followers, we are called to be a *light*, a visible display that helps those who are estranged from God to find Him. We must relate to this world in a way that draws other people to Him. What does it mean to shine as lights? The answer is a very tangible one: do good works that are genuine and remarkable enough to cause others to glorify our Father in heaven. This command has three parts:

- Substance: good works
- Exposure: that people can see
- Result: glorifying God

Substance

Let's break each part down, starting with the substance of genuine and remarkable "good works." Jesus asked us to join Him in His redemptive work to heal the brokenness in this world. When He returns someday, He will complete that good work. Until then, He uses the church as His movement of radical love to bring restoration and reconciliation. The closer we follow Him, the more we will en-

---

[1] Matthew 5:14-16, NIV.

gage our culture with genuine good works that make the world better and draw people to the Father.

Our culture is hungry for such redemption because most people feel the brokenness of our world. Right now, non-believers often perceive that the church contributes to the brokenness rather than bringing wholeness, but that can change if we jump on board with Jesus's good work.

At our church, we have found that doing so has drawn us deeper and deeper into real, substantive, and effective good work that makes an appreciable difference. Virtually everyone in our culture values doing good. Who doesn't want our world to be a better place? People buy socks, sunglasses, shoes, and purses that give back to third-world initiatives. They post slogans on social media to show how committed they are to ending various injustices and aiding those who face poverty, disease, and disaster. I'm all for it, even though much of it is more "talk" than it is real, effective, "good work" that eventuates in real change. But I think most people know that and would love to be part of something that is more substantive.

That's where the church comes in as part of Jesus's redemptive mission. He invites us to join Him in His truly good and substantive work. Our church has been experiencing an ongoing journey of deepening our understanding of and involvement in that good work. Years ago, our church adopted a more external focus, and we began to engage with the needs of our community and world. It was a good start. We addressed the symptoms of poverty in our community by asking our people to provide food, clothing, medical care, school supplies, and other forms of charity to alleviate the critical needs of others. That's all really good, and there's a place for that. We still do all of those things, but as our engagement deepened, so did our understanding of the deeper needs that keep people in poverty. With our city leaders and other community partners, we began to address not only the symptoms of poverty but also the underlying causes and constraints that keep people there. Eventually, we started what is now called "The Local Good Center" to address those deeper needs. We hope to pull people out of poverty by helping them to bridge the chasm. We provide advocacy, jobs, training, nutrition, and mentorship to move people toward a life of sustainable flourishing. We also realize that we can't do this alone, so we partner closely with our city and other organizations. Every day, we get more deeply involved in Jesus's redemptive work. It's real. It's costly. It's difficult. It's confusing at times. And it's really, really good!

I have found that many people outside the church value substantive community transformation, which churches are uniquely positioned to accomplish. A current leader in our church started as a skeptical non-believer who saw the tangible work being done by our church. She heard about all that was going on and asked a neighbor who led a small group if she could contribute to the cause. I loved the way she asked: "I really want to be part of what your church is doing, but I don't want to go to church. I don't want to be converted or have anyone attempt to convert me. I will never go to a church service, and I don't want anyone to ask. In essence, I'd like to use the church as a means to get what I want: the opportunity to make a difference in a real way. I completely understand why you might say no, but that's what I'm asking." Her neighbor invited her to serve with the group, and eventually she did get pulled into a relationship with Jesus and into the life of the church. The substantive and holistic good works that our world hopes for are best found in Jesus's ongoing mission.

Exposure

The substance of our good works is the most important element, but Jesus told us to engage in a way that people can see. If we hope to change people's perceptions toward a God they don't yet know, then we must do good works in a way that they can see. People are hungry to see something real and good, and we need to help them experience it.

I was struck by the power of this idea a couple of years ago while watching online church. I was watching with a small group of church people and one non-churched person who had watched our online church services multiple times. After some music, the announcer began to make the weekly announcements, and those of us who were church regulars did what most church regulars do during the announcements: we tuned out. We started talking to each other about something else. What happened next was so surprising to me. The non-churched member of our watch party had the remote, and she pushed pause. She looked at the rest of us and said, "Do you mind not talking during this part of the service? It's my favorite part." As the pastor who does most of the teaching, I kind of hoped that my sermons were her favorite part. But nope! She preferred the announcements. Now chided, we all got quiet. She pressed play again and was completely focused on every word. After the service, I asked her why the announcements were her favorite part. She said, "Oh! I love your part too, but the announcements are when you talk about what the church is doing to make your community better. It's always intriguing to me, and I love it. People in my generation are great at talking about what's important to us, but you guys are actually moving the needle. That's what I want to hear about and be a part of." I realized that the best invitation to her—and maybe most people—is not "come to church," but "come change the world with us." This conversation certainly changed the way I view that part of the service, but it also helped me understand Jesus's command to be a light.

Jesus told His followers to do good works in a way people can see so that they can be pulled in. Two thousand years ago, when most people lived in villages, this wasn't that hard to do. Christians would do genuine good works, and people walking by could see. As people passed the stories on, word got out. Doing good works was part of normal life for the early Christians, and their reputation spread through word of mouth.

Today, we can certainly still count on word of mouth, but we have many more tools at our disposal to help people see our genuine good works. We have many effective forms of media that can expose people to the goodness of Jesus at work. Here are a few ways that we have attempted to better engage those we are trying to reach:

Media agencies. Our church decided to invest in two different media agencies that would help us better communicate to our community. We purposely chose secular agencies because we wanted people outside the church to tell us how we could best connect to others outside the church. This tactic has been wildly effective in connecting our good works to our community, in growing the reputation of Jesus, and in helping us learn how to better communicate with those who are dismissive of Christians. One company was very dubious about working with us because they didn't want to help people who would make the world worse. From what they knew about large churches, they assumed that we would fall into that category. However, as they spent time vetting us, they were shocked by the goodness of Jesus expressed in and through our community. They soon decided that helping people connect to this movement of radical good might be the most important work they will ever do.

The Good Complex. One of the media agencies proposed that we start a podcast to feature the good things happening in Christianity and to provide a space in this polarized world where we can have civil and helpful conversations about complex issues. In a world so full of fear, vitriol, and bad news, we wanted to provide a space full of hope, encouragement, and good news. The podcast's target audience is not Christians, but those several layers outside of Christianity who have no exposure to the good works of Christians. Check it out at thegoodcomplex.com!

Campaigns. Many churches host successful community engagement campaigns that provide easy entry for people who want to make a difference in their communities. North Point Church in Atlanta conducts a "Be Rich" campaign every year, which asks people to give or serve in tangible, inclusive, and relatively easy ways. Campaigns like this also provide great opportunities to invite non-churched friends to participate.

We have also engaged our people through similar campaigns to serve those outside the church. One of my personal favorites was the "Love Does the Unexpected" campaign, which was all about showing love in unexpected ways. The idea was to find those who felt the least loved by the church and demonstrate love to them in surprising ways. One group we focused on was the LGBTQ+ community. We found an incredible organization, the AIDS Association of Dallas, that cares for those in the last stages of HIV/AIDS. They provide housing, medical care, community, food—everything. We found that most people who care for that community are themselves LGBTQ+—but Jesus cares even more, and we are His followers. We knew that we had to engage if they would let us (which was a process). Raising money in a campaign and writing a big check is easy, but personally involving our people in loving this community was a little different. This community didn't know our church, and being part of a care network for people who already felt so much fear and rejection was scary. They didn't associate Christians with radical love, but radical judgment. However, as we started engaging, they experienced unexpected love. They were not only surprised but also intrigued enough to deepen the conversation and gain a fuller understanding of who we are as Christians.

Let's get creative and use every available tool to help people see the good works that Jesus is doing in our world. If we do, I think we will be surprised by the results. This leads us into the next part of Jesus's command.

Result

We shouldn't do good works just to make other people feel good. And we shouldn't do them to make ourselves feel better. It's important to remember the intended result of the good works: to help people connect with the divine brand and to help them see that God is way more loving and glorious than they can imagine. This will happen if we join Him in His movement of radical love in real, tangible ways.

Unfortunately, many people in our culture see Christians as bad people who do bad things and make our world worse. I suppose that one positive result of their low expectations is that it doesn't take much to surprise them with the genuine love of Jesus! We saw that with our "Love Does the Unexpected" campaign as illustrated above. Some members of their board became curious enough that they planned to attend a church service to find out why we seemed so different from other Christians they'd met. They called to let us know that they were planning to come. Ironically, I was going to be speaking on sexuality—specifically how we, members of a church with a traditionally Christian view of sexuality (sex is designed to take place within marriage between a man and woman), should show love to the LBGTQ+ community. When I found out that they were coming, I thought, "Really? This weekend of all weekends?"

When they arrived, one of our pastors met them in the parking lot and asked, "When you go to church, where do you like to sit?"

The board chairman said, "Where would I like to sit if I go to church? The parking lot!" Nevertheless, they did go in, and they heard not only about our commitment to a biblical view of sexuality, but also about our commitment to love people no matter what. When they came up to thank me after the service, they were so enthusiastic. One of them said, "We know where you're coming from, but we also know that we are welcome and loved here. If I went to church, I would choose this one." He then briefly shared a story of significant church hurt from his past. He was thankful that a faith community like ours existed, and I could tell that he left the service glorifying our Father in heaven a little bit.

People are so tired of the brokenness in this world and so ready to be part of genuine change. Jesus wants us to join Him in being the answer people are looking for, which will in turn draw people to the Father. Putting love into action has always been the most powerful way for the church to win over a skeptical world.

What if people thought of Christians in the same way that they think about the Salvation Army? They might think that the folks with the Salvation Army are a little strange (uniforms and everything), but at the same time, they must be thankful for those kinds of people in our world—people who care for others, sacrifice themselves, and "do the most good." They may not be ready to put on the uniform, but they are thankful for the work being done, especially when they are the recipients of such care. What people in our culture thought of Christians similarly: "I don't understand everything they say, and they sing some funny songs, but I would hate to live in this broken world without them. They are amazing. They do the most good of anyone we know, so we're thankful that they are on this planet." That's the idea that would win over our world and cause many people to glorify our Father in heaven.

10

THE WIDEST WELCOME

One of the most common charges that the emerging generations make against Christianity is that our welcome is narrow and that we reject those who are unlike us. The irony, however, is that a wide welcome should be one of our greatest strengths because that would reflect the heritage and spirit of our Founder.

Jesus's form of hospitality welcomed all people into relationship with Him, especially those who were marginalized. This wide welcome often got Him into hot water with the religious elite who confused acceptance with approval. He was always eating, drinking, and associating with all the wrong people, earning Him the derisive title of "friend of sinners and tax collectors."

Isn't it interesting how religious people, who are sinners themselves, love to label others who sin differently with the title of *sinner*? And isn't it interesting how each generation of religious people has its own group that gets singled out and becomes the unwelcome guest at the table?

In Jesus's day, that group was tax collectors, a fact that may seem kind of ridiculous to us now. Don't get me wrong—I'm no fan of paying taxes (so much so that I typically wait until the absolute last minute to file them). I don't, however, view IRS agents as the worst of humanity. We even hired an IRS agent to be one of our campus pastors, so there! To us, it may seem bizarre that tax collectors were the singled-out group back then, even if we understand the historical reasons why they were particularly hated.

Yet, someone from two thousand years ago might find it completely bizarre that Christians today tend to single out and reject the LGBTQ+ community. Why would someone struggling with their gender identity or sexual orientation feel like church is the last place they would be accepted? Regardless of who gets singled out in a particular generation, we should pay attention to the way in which Jesus modeled a wide welcome, which often included eating and drinking in the homes of "the wrong people." Jesus knew what a strong statement He was making because in His day, table fellowship sent a strong social message. New Testament scholar Scott Bartchy writes:

> It would be difficult to overestimate the importance of table fellowship for the cultures of the . . . first century. . . . Mealtimes were far more than occasions for individuals to [eat]. Being welcomed at a table for the purpose of eating food with another person had become a ceremony richly symbolic of friendship, intimacy and unity. Thus betrayal or unfaithfulness toward anyone with whom one had shared the table was viewed as particularly

reprehensible. On the other hand, when persons were estranged, a meal invitation opened the way to reconciliation.[1]

I love the way John Mark Comer expresses Jesus's way of relating: *"Jesus's mission was to seek and save the lost and His method was to eat and drink with people. Jesus saved people one meal at a time!"[2]*

Jesus not only modeled such hospitality and welcome, but He also taught us to live the same way around our own tables. At a dinner party where He was sharing table fellowship with religious elites, He issued this challenge:

"When you put on a luncheon or a banquet," he said, "don't invite your friends, brothers, relatives, and rich neighbors. For they will invite you back, and that will be your only reward. Instead, invite the poor, the crippled, the lame, and the blind. Then at the resurrection of the righteous, God will reward you for inviting those who could not repay you.[3]

For Jesus, the best dinner party was one with culture's most marginalized, including those who were poor and also those who were considered especially sinful.

When the church was born, radical hospitality was a tangible expression of God's love, and it remains a key indicator of Jesus's brand. The church was an expression of God's family, into which

---

[1] S.S. Bartchy, "Table Fellowship," in *Dictionary of Jesus and the Gospels*, edited by Joel B. Green and Scot McKnight (Downer's Grove: IVP Press, 1992), 796.
[2] Lawrence, Matt. "Radical Hospitality: Around a Table." ragamuffinreflections, June 9, 2020. https://ragamuffinreflections.wordpress.com/2020/06/09/radical-hospitality-around-a-table/#:~:text=And%20John%20Mark%20Comer%20says,it%20in%20verses%201%2D10.
[3] Luke 14:12-14, NLT.

all were welcomed with open arms. The writer of Hebrews gave this challenge to the church:

> *"Keep on loving each other as brothers and sisters. Don't forget to show hospitality to strangers, for some who have done this have entertained angels without realizing it!"*[4]

The Greek word translated *hospitality* is simply two words put together: *philos* ("love") and *xenos* ("stranger"). Hospitality expresses love to those who are unlike us by accepting them into our lives—to our table, so to speak. The same word is used in Titus 1:8: for someone to become an elder in the church, they must live like Jesus by welcoming those who are way different than themselves. Peter also instructs the church:

> *"Above all, love each other deeply, because love covers over a multitude of sins. Offer hospitality to one another without grumbling."*[5]

When gathered together and when scattered out into our neighborhoods and workplaces, Christians are to love strangers and widely welcome everyone. This kind of wide welcome was so rare in the Roman world that it was part of what won that world over for Jesus.

The early church did not always get it right, however. They happily enjoyed the practice of regular communal meals (including the Lord's Supper) where all were welcome around the table—sinners and strugglers, rich and poor, doubters and believers. But Paul became very angry with the Corinthian church when they began to

---

[4] Hebrews 13:1-2, NLT.
[5] 1 Peter 4:8-9, NIV.

exclude the poor and marginalized from their regular table fellowship. Paul considered this to be one of the most offensive sins they could commit as a church. They were sinning against the body of Christ in the worst possible way.[6] Everyone is welcome at God's table, so church should be the one place where everybody knows that they will be accepted and loved. Church should be the place where every path leads to an open door of acceptance, where we can walk with each other into the life that Jesus wants for us.

Sadly, this is often not the case, and the watching world knows it. Do you remember the excluded group in our time—the LGBTQ+ community? A recent Gallup study found that while only 5.6 percent of the American population identifies as LGBTQ+, 15.9 percent of Gen Z identifies that way.[7] This means that one sixth of Gen Z identify as LGBTQ+, and virtually 100 percent have friends who do. No wonder they care so deeply about the way the LGBTQ+ community is treated. According to another study, 71 percent of young people claimed to greatly value how LGBTQ+ people are regarded, and only 44 percent felt like faith communities share that same value.[8] For many, the church tops the list of those who mistreat the LGBTQ+ community, and many within that community feel like the church is the last place they can go to find acceptance.

A few years ago, I preached a sermon called, "Why did God make me gay and then say I can't be that way?" I am no prophet, but I bet that you have several reactions to the wording of that question

---

[6] See 1 Corinthians 11:20-22.
[7] Jones, Jeffrey M. "LGBT Identification Rises to 5.6% in Latest U.S. Estimate," Gallup, February 24, 2021, https://news.gallup.com/poll/329708/lgbt-identification-rises-latest-estimate.aspx.
[8] *The State of Religion and Young People* (Springtide Research Institute, 2021).

bouncing around in your head right now. I get it. The title came from a real question I received from someone on social media after soliciting questions for a sermon series built around what people wanted us to address. The title is provocative enough that the talk gets many YouTube views, including from those in the gay community. Many of them reach out to me, and the most common question I get is, "As a gay person, could I really come to your church and be accepted?" If they live out of town, they will ask if such a church might exist where they live. The question is incredibly sad to me because the one place that any person should know for certain they would be accepted is church. There is room for everyone around Jesus's table.

However, this might seem tricky for a church like mine, which is not an "affirming" church. This means that we maintain a belief in the biblical view of sex and marriage: that sex is for marriage, and marriage is between one man and one woman. Regardless, we still accept everyone as they are, even if they never agree with our point of view. We accept people as they are and point them to what Jesus affirms as a better way to live. There is no sin in being same-sex attracted or struggling with gender identity; rather, it's what we do with our attractions or struggles that can be sinful. We believe that the best place to work all that out is within Christian community. The most important thing is that people meet Jesus, and then we can walk together toward what He teaches. That is a process for all of us, regardless of our orientation or struggle, and it takes space and time. Grace gives us both. This reminds me of Henri Nouwen's wonderful description of hospitality:

Hospitality means primarily the creation of free space where the stranger can enter and become a friend instead of an enemy. Hospitality is not to change people but to offer them space where change can take place. It is not to bring men and women over to our side, but to offer freedom not disturbed by dividing lines.[9]

The Christian community seems to have no problem accepting and patiently journeying alongside those with other issues, but LGBTQ+ triggers unkindness and rejection for many. I experienced this firsthand after being "canceled" by many Christians for simply welcoming the gay and transgender community to my church's fellowship table. For the last couple of years, we have had the privilege of hosting a conference called Revoice, which is put on by an organization with the same name. Revoice exists to help those in the LGBTQ+ community find and follow Jesus, which includes pointing them to a traditional sexual ethic as affirmed by Jesus. This means that same-sex attracted make a great sacrifice by surrendering the sexual part of their lives to the lordship of Christ and living a single, celibate life or in a mixed orientation marriage.

I've been overwhelmed and saddened by the response of so many Evangelical Christians to such an event. The idea that someone could even be a "gay Christian" is seen as blasphemous. I've been particularly shocked by the slanderous accusations against the Revoice leadership and participants (which you can easily find on various blogs and podcasts from people who I suppose make their living by slandering

---

[9] "Hospitality," Henri Nouwen Society, February 18, 2021, https://henrinouwen.org/meditations/hospitality/#:~:text=Hospitality%20means%20primarily%20the%20creation,where%20change%20can%20take%20place.

other Christians). Some of that unwanted attention has been aimed at me and my church as well. I am not gay, but I am a very public friend of those who are. Based on the small amount of vitriol that has come my way, I can understand why I get so many questions from LGBTQ+ people wondering if they could ever show up at a church and be welcomed to the party.

Can a non-affirming church be an accepting church? I hope so. That's how Jesus lived His life and how He calls us to live ours. If we don't get this right, we will continue to shove away people Jesus loves and earn a reputation of being mean to those who are already marginalized and mistreated.

The church's relationship with those outside the church and the emerging generations within the church is in jeopardy. Consider what Bruce Miller posits:

> *Deep inside, people raised as Christians realize something about churches not warmly welcoming LGBTQ+ people can't be right. Sadly, that inner discomfort leads some to deconstruct their entire Christian faith. If the church is wrong about not embracing gay and trans people, maybe it's wrong about the whole Christian faith. Is Jesus really God as he claims to be? Is the Bible a reliable document? Is there even a God, at least as Christianity describes him? In the public sphere, Christianity's appeal is diminished by its apparent rejection of LGBTQ+ people. Who wants to join a group that hates marginalized people? . . . Could we not return to the founder Jesus' original message and model? Could Christians reconstruct their faith in Christ-like ways full of grace*

and truth? Could churches become loving, diverse communities where everyone is welcome?[10]

These are such great questions, and we must do better with the answers. On the positive side, imagine if we did! In a world where acceptance equals approval, what if we modeled a different way forward? What if we could accept people with stories and points of view that are strange to us? Imagine if we could be stranger-lovers and sinner-lovers who welcome everyone with warm hospitality? Imagine if the church was the one place where every single person knew they would be welcomed, loved, accepted, and embraced in a common pursuit of Jesus. That is church as Jesus intended, and He invites us to join Him in living out that dream.

---

[10] Miller, Bruce, "Lamenting the church's historic rejection of LGBTQ people," Dallas Morning News, December 10, 2022.

11

RULES OF ENGAGEMENT

The way we say something is just as important as what we say. I can change the meaning of my words just by changing my tone. For example, I could say, "You are so smart," in a positive tone or a sarcastic one, and I would convey a different meaning each time. Even my dog Chewie, a very cute Yorkie mix, understands this reality perfectly. He reacts differently when I say, "Come here!" in an angry tone than when I say it in a happy one. The former causes him to run and hide, and the latter causes him to run toward me with his tail wagging with anticipation.

As Christians, we have important things to say. We believe that God has revealed truth that leads to better lives and opportunities for connection to our Creator. Our responsibility to authentically live out Jesus's brand in a way that creates curiosity and openness to Him means not only that we have something to share but also that we must be very careful how we share it. The way we engage with people will in large part determine how they respond back.

Of course, this is not new for Christians in culture; Jesus and the apostles often encouraged Christians to be careful about how we engage with those who we're called to love. As a maligned minority tasked with winning over a hostile world, the early Christians faced a much more difficult task than we do today. However, we are experiencing a unique cultural moment, and we need to be guided by the same commands.

We've talked a lot in this book about how often people are on the edge of outrage and how Christians have often contributed to the problem. There's no need to keep beating that horse, but a key reason why our culture is either running away from us or coming against us aggressively is the same reason why my dog Chewie runs and hides. We must change our tone if we hope to gain a hearing and model Christlike civility. I've had hundreds of conversations about what's going on in our culture with both Christians and non-Christians, all of whom lament the loss of civility in public discourse. Everyone hopes that the tone will shift.

Paul told the Colossian Christians to *"Live wisely among those who are not believers, and make the most of every opportunity. Let your conversation be gracious and attractive so that you will have the right response for everyone."*[1] We must engage carefully, wisely, and winsomely so that we don't miss opportunities for positive impact. We may be frustrated with how others perceive us, but we can work to improve those negative perceptions. The New Testament describes how to act with civility and relate to others in a way that makes

[1] Colossians 4:5-6, NLT.

people more inclined to engage with us. I'll summarize the instructions under three core commands that are essential to civil and attractive engagement.

Choose Humility

Humility is *the* core component of civil engagement. David Brooks, a social commentator and columnist for *The New York Times*, has spent much of his career focusing on the restoration of civil discourse. In a column that caused a very positive stir in 2011, he wrote:

> *So this is where civility comes from—from a sense of personal modesty and from the ensuing gratitude for the political process. Civility is the natural state for people who know how limited their own individual powers are and know, too, that they need the conversation. They are useless without the conversation.*
>
> *The problem is that over the past 40 years or so we have gone from a culture that reminds people of their own limitations to a culture that encourages people to think highly of themselves. The nation's founders had a modest but realistic opinion of themselves and of the voters. They erected all sorts of institutional and social restraints to protect Americans from themselves. They admired George Washington because of the way he kept himself in check.*
>
> *But over the past few decades, people have lost a sense of their own sinfulness. Children are raised amid a chorus of applause. Politics has become less about institutional restraint and more about giving voters whatever they want at that second. Joe DiMaggio didn't ostentatiously admire his own home runs,*

but now athletes routinely celebrate themselves as part of the self-branding process.

So, of course, you get narcissists who believe they or members of their party possess direct access to the truth. Of course you get people who prefer monologue to dialogue. Of course you get people who detest politics because it frustrates their ability to get 100 percent of what they want. Of course you get people who gravitate toward the like-minded and loathe their political opponents. They feel no need for balance and correction.

Beneath all the other things that have contributed to polarization and the loss of civility, the most important is this: The roots of modesty have been carved away.[2]

What he calls *modesty*, the Bible calls *humility*, an essential component of civil public engagement. One of the biblical principles that influenced our Founding Fathers was the belief that humans are fallible and therefore must humbly realize their need for different points of view. The Founding Fathers developed the two party system according to this very idea. Government—and any human institution—can only be truly effective if people are humble enough to listen to other perspectives and recognize that opposing ideas are a very valuable gift.[3] Without humility, human systems cannot function.

Paul instructed Christians to lead the way in humility as we engage with others. He told the Ephesian Christians to *"be completely*

---

[2] Brooks, David, "Tree of Failure," The New York Times, January 13, 2011, https://www.nytimes.com/2011/01/14/opinion/14brooks.html.
[3] Ben Sasse, *Them: Why We Hate Each Other—and How to Heal* (New York: St Martin's Griffin, 2019).

humble and gentle.[4] He told the believers on Crete that they should avoid contentiousness and *"instead . . . be gentle and show true humility to everyone."*[5] Note that he said *true,* not fake, and *everyone,* not just those who agree with you or who are humble themselves. *Everyone* is perhaps the hardest part of the command.

Thirty or so years ago, when I was a very confident young adult leader, I had a formative conversation with one of my life mentors, pastor and author Gene Getz. I can't remember the public figure I was calling out as being completely ridiculous, but I enjoyed sharing my critique of how "out to lunch" he was. I expected Gene to be so impressed with me and to jump on my bandwagon of complete rejection of all this person had to say. Instead, he simply said, "You know, Jeff, I've learned that if I listen to someone enough, regardless of who they are, I can usually find something helpful in what they have to say. They may not be right about everything, but they're usually right about something." This was his way of saying, "Show true humility to everyone."

Similarly, Dwight Jewson, a contributor to this book, has challenged me to grow in humility while impressing upon me its necessity in a civil world. He has used his branding expertise to help major political campaigns at the highest level, but he recently stopped his political engagement because things have gotten so unreasonably contentious and partisan. Humility is a life commitment for him, and he tried to instill that in the politicians he tried to help.

---

[4] Ephesians 4:2, NIV.
[5] Titus 3:2, NLT.

He offers this challenge: "Even when talking with those who are your most stark ideological opposites, listen to them long enough until you can answer the question, 'Where are they right?'" Until he can answer that question, he knows that he has not engaged with the other person long enough.

Dwight's challenge mirrors James 1:19: "*You must all be quick to listen, slow to speak, and slow to get angry*" (NLT). Imagine if we operated this way. Instead of reacting quickly to something that stokes our anger, what if we chose to listen? Instead of focusing so much on being heard, what if we slowed down enough to actually listen—even if we disagree?

It's amazing what can happen when we're humble enough to listen to those who are different than us. First, we gain insight that we never could have gained on our own. Second, we often find common ground with those who see things differently; we may find that we don't disagree on everything and can work together to pursue the common good. Third, developing relationships with other types of people helps to shatter our stereotypes about them.

In 2020, our church launched multiple small groups in which people committed to gather for meals with others who did not look like them. The idea was to provide a safe place for people from different ethnic backgrounds to interact and share stories of what it's like to live in this culture. It's astounding what can happen over a meal conversation. What I noticed, though, is that while most people really benefited from the experience and felt like their eyes were opened in significant ways, others felt like their time was wasted.

Further dialogue revealed the difference: those who were humble and sought to understand others' perspectives benefited greatly, whereas those who were more focused on speaking than listening ended up not benefiting at all. When we are humble enough to listen and learn, we contribute to our culture becoming more unified and less divided.

Be Gracious

Since Christians understand the innate dignity of every human being created in God's image, we should be the most respectful and gracious people on the planet—and we are called to be. We already saw this command in Colossians: *"Let your conversation be gracious and attractive so that you will have the right response for everyone."*[6] Peter told the Christians in Rome (who were facing persecution) to "respect everyone."[7] Again we see the word *everyone*, and in this case, it even referred to their persecutors. The early Christians faced significant opposition, much of which was completely unfair and malicious, but the New Testament's consistent and frequent command was to respond graciously, gently, and respectfully.

This kind of response is surprising, especially in a world full of outrage. The New Testament is clear that we are not to react in anger or participate in quarreling, but we are to love and respect those who oppose us instead. Consider Paul's command to Timothy: *"Again I say, don't get involved in foolish, ignorant arguments that only start fights. A servant of the Lord must not quarrel but must*

---

[6] Colossians 4:6, NLT.
[7] 1 Peter 2:17, NLT.

be kind to everyone, be able to teach, and be patient with difficult people. Gently instruct those who oppose the truth. Perhaps God will change those people's hearts, and they will learn the truth.[8] Paul also told the believers in Ephesus to *"get rid of all bitterness, rage, anger, harsh words, and slander, as well as all types of evil behavior."*[9] Rage may be common in our culture, but Jesus followers should not be spewing flames of vitriol.

This is easier said than done, especially on social media. Social media seems designed to cause fights (in fact, recent whistleblower revelations have revealed that this is actually one of Facebook's business strategies to keep users engaged). I'm amazed by what people say on social media that they would never say to someone's face. Studies have shown that the sense of anonymity provided by platforms like Facebook empowers people to be far meaner and more disrespectful than they would ever dare to be in person. My wife occasionally reads me posts on NextDoor, some of which are great. Yet, it is also clear that we have several very grumpy neighbors, as indicated by disrespectful comments on posts that seem so innocuous. It's like people just have their fingers on the verbal trigger and are always ready to shoot.

When Christians who post Bible verses, worship songs, and pictures of community service also post harsh or mean-spirited content, the incongruence feels hypocritical to those outside of our faith, and rightly so. Instead, we should be coming to people's rescue when they are disrespected on social media, and we should never share an unkind comment.

---

[8] 2 Timothy 2:23-25, NLT.
[9] Ephesians 4:31, NLT.

Rather than contributing to the outrage of our culture, our engagement should always be characterized by graciousness to everyone. The New Testament uses these words to guide our cultural interactions: Kind. Respectful. Gentle. Patient. Humble. Forgiving. Compassionate. We should always take the high road, and as we do, we will win the respect of others and make them interested in what we have to say.

Bill Henson is a friend of mine who modeled this well. He was asked to speak to a group at Case Western University on a controversial topic. The event sparked a great deal of angst on the campus, and when he arrived, fifty or so protestors were gathered outside, holding disparaging signs and shouting loud remarks. I love what Bill chose to do. Instead of reacting with anger and fighting back, or just retreating inside, he went out to the group and said, "Hey, I can tell that you're really upset, and you probably have good reason to be. I'd love to hear what you have to say so that I can understand." With that, the tone completely shifted, and protestors began to share their stories. Many of them had been hurt by Christians in the past. Bill listened, empathized with their pain, cried with them, apologized, and assured them that he was just there to love people. As a result, they put down their signs, some hugged and thanked him, and others joined the event they came to protest with an open posture. His choice was not complicated; he did what Jesus always did and simply treated them with grace and dignity.

Avoid Slander

Throughout the Bible, God shares what He hates. You might think that cats made the list, but no—they never did. What consistently *did* make the list, however, was slander (or bearing false witness). In one such passage, Paul urged Titus to guide believers' cultural engagement in this way: *"They must not slander anyone and must avoid quarreling. Instead, they should be gentle and show true humility to everyone."*[10]

Slander is simply sharing untrue things about someone else. If you've ever been slandered, you know how unfair and damaging it is. God hates it for the same reason. With so many forms of media that exist now, slander is more ubiquitous than ever, and I'm quite sure this frustrates God—particularly when His people are doing the slandering.

Consider all the conspiracy theories that are spread on Facebook, often by Christians. Recently, the *MIT Technology Review* published internal documents that were leaked from Facebook and showed that in 2019, nearly half of Americans had connected with untrue content produced by troll farms in Eastern Europe and designed to further divide our country.[11] The three targeted groups were African Americans, Native Americans, and Christians. The Christian-targeted pages reached around 75 million people each month and were by far the most commonly read Christian pages on Facebook. Nineteen of the top twenty Christian Facebook pages were illegitimate,

---

[10] Titus 3:2, NLT.
[11] Hao, Karen, "Troll Farms Reached 140 Million Americans a Month on Facebook, Internal Report Shows," MIT Technology Review, September 16, 2021.

and they propagated complete untruths to kindle Christians' outrage against other groups. Unfortunately, many Christians not only believed them but also felt obligated to share them widely. Of course, Christians aren't the only ones who get manipulated, but we must be way more careful than we have been.

Both on and off social media, we must be careful to know the truth before making false judgments about organizations, the government, and individuals. In my own community a few years ago, the mayor and city officials decided to include the LGBTQ+ community in their anti-discrimination policies. Immediately, a number of churches and Christian political action groups rallied to take a stand in favor of truth and against what the city leaders were attempting to do. They organized press releases and communicated that the city was, among other things, opening bathrooms to transgender people, which could cause terrible things to happen to children in those bathrooms. They also shared that these policies would force Christian organizations to hire candidates who don't share their sexual ethic.

Since my church partners with the city leaders for the good of the community, I knew the mayor and other officials. So, I called and asked what they were trying to accomplish. They explained that they weren't doing what was being communicated; instead, they were simply trying to protect the rights of community members in ways that most cities had already implemented. It had nothing to do with bathrooms, and they wanted to make sure that they also protected the freedoms of religious organizations to hire within their ethical beliefs. They asked if I would help with the language to protect religious freedom while also helping people understand that their measures were about protecting another group just as they wanted to protect Christians. They also asked for help in calming down the faith community by sharing what was happening. The mayor organized a meeting with several local pastors, and he asked our executive pastor to help moderate the conversation. Afterwards, the faith leaders who had reacted so strongly apologized for overreacting and agreed to stop characterizing the policy falsely. I hope they also apologized to their church bodies and clarified the reality that they had misconstrued, but at least they took responsibility with the mayor and stopped spreading slander. This incident provided an embarrassing example of how easily we can slander people when we react before knowing the facts.

We must be so careful before making judgments, and we should refrain from doing so until we actually know what's going on. It's too easy for anyone, Christian or not, to make judgments about other people, especially if they disagree with us or we don't like them. We can't know people's motives, so instead of making judgment calls, we should do what Jesus commands us to do: love people. When we love people, 1 Corinthians 13 lets us know that we will believe the best about them. When we don't understand someone's motives, let's assume the best. In a world that is so sloppy about slander, we cannot be. Our commitment must be to slander no one. When we don't know, we should assume the best rather than the worst.

Let's put all of this together. Love's rules of engagement direct us to choose humility, be gracious always, and slander no one. We can engage with others wisely and winsomely, which will be incredibly refreshing in a world where civility seems to be extinct. Tone really does matter, which is why the New Testament speaks so much about it. Let's give Paul the last word: *"Live wisely among those who are not believers, and make the most of every opportunity. Let your conversation be gracious and attractive so that you will have the right response for everyone."*[12]

---

[12] Colossians 4:5-6, NLT.

Case Study: iPhone—Someone Is Always Watching

In the movie *Ocean's 11*, there is a scene in which Tess Ocean (Julia Roberts) says to Terry Benedict (Andy Garcia), "You of all people should know, Terry, in your hotel, there's always someone watching."[13] While I'm certain this is true in casinos, I'm equally confident that it also applies to the world of branding. Everyone watches—your customers, your competitors, your employees. This is truer today than ever before, and it's changing the way we live. Think about these examples:

- **iPhone:** How many of us watched the video of George Floyd's arrest in Minneapolis? Seventeen-year-old Darnella Frazier captured the video on her iPhone, which sparked widespread outrage and ultimately helped to convict Officer Derek Chauvin. In cities across the US, police reports used to provide the "official" versions of what happened. Now, everyone is free to film their own version and post it for millions to see.

- **Glassdoor:** Glassdoor is an online-based company that specializes in collecting employee reviews of companies. If you want to know about employee satisfaction or even how much certain positions pay, just look on Glassdoor. This information used to be considered

---

[13] *Ocean's 11*, directed by Steven Soderbergh (2001; Warner Brothers).

confidential, but now employers have no control over what is said.

This is called *transparency*, and it's here to stay. It is extremely dangerous to play by the old rules, as the following story illustrates:

- The HBO documentary *The Jinx* tells the story of Robert Durst, a man suspected of multiple murders. During the filming of the documentary and before his trial, Durst confessed to the killings while in the bathroom—not realizing that his microphone was still on. The recording was used at the trial, and it led to his conviction.

Unfortunately, negative things seem to travel much farther and faster than positive ones. Research suggests that unhappy customers will tell an average of ten to fifteen other people about their experience. Generating even a small number of negative experiences can seriously hurt a brand's long-term success. Smart brands have figured this out. It is certainly the case that negative experiences are multiplied, but it is also true that sincere recommendations from your brand's "fans" are the most valuable form of marketing. People value what they hear from peers far more than what they hear from "experts." People who used to read professional movie or restaurant reviews now regularly reference Rotten Tomatoes or Yelp.

Entire businesses have been built on this movement. Think about companies like Uber or VRBO. Their businesses rely overwhelmingly on consumer reviews. Why would I entrust my vacation to a private rental rather than sticking with a well-known and highly regulated brand like Hilton? The answer is because I have grown to trust the peer-to-peer reviews of VRBO more than the brand Hilton. I know I'm getting unfiltered feedback from people who have been in my situation.

What key principles apply to the church?
Remember that people are always watching.

- Generally speaking, they are looking to see if our actions are consistent with our words.

- We have a great opportunity to be consistent and to challenge ourselves to put our beliefs into action.

- The more we consistently follow through with our promises (for example, by doing good in our communities), the more opportunities we create for people to "catch us doing good."

12

MEANT TO BE HATED

If you are familiar with Jesus's sayings about how His people will be hated by the world, you've probably been feeling tense as you've read this book. Jesus told His followers:

> *If the world hates you, remember that it hated me first. The world would love you as one of its own if you belonged to it, but you are no longer part of the world. I chose you to come out of the world, so it hates you. Do you remember what I told you? "A slave is not greater than the master." Since they persecuted me, naturally they will persecute you.*[1]

Here's the tension: If we're supposed to represent Jesus in a winsome way (as many of the passages in the New Testament suggest), how does that mesh with what Jesus said about being hated? Am I using this book to say that we should try to be liked when Jesus said that won't happen?

---
[1] John 15:18-20, NLT.

This is a great tension, and I think it's one worth living with. However, let's clarify some things. First, the goal is not to be liked; the goal is to be faithful to Jesus's commands and love like He loved so that people experience His love for them. The goal is to authentically reflect Jesus to people, to love radically and selflessly.

The truth is that radical love is subversive. It upsets the power structures of religion and other worldly systems. It's no accident that Jesus was hated by the religious establishment but loved by the marginalized (including the sick, the poor, the sinners, and the tax collectors). It's no accident that the Roman emperors felt threatened by the Christian movement, but the populace was won over by the Christians' expressions of love both within their community and outside of it. Jesus-style love is powerfully disruptive, and not everyone will appreciate it. But our goal is not to be liked; it's to authentically live out the Jesus brand as He gave it.

Second, we need to do all we can to ensure that any rejection, hatred, or even persecution is happening for the right reasons. Peter said just that when talking to Christian slaves in the Roman world.[2] He said if they were mistreated because they were doing wrong, that was on them. However, if they were mistreated for doing what's right, then they would be identifying with Jesus who experienced the same suffering, and they would be rewarded later for enduring the unfair treatment. In the next chapter, he restated the principle for everyone: *"Now, who will harm you if you are eager to do good? But even if you suffer for doing what is right, God will reward you for it. So don't worry or be afraid of their threats."*[3]

---

[2] See 1 Peter 2:20-23, NLT.
[3] 1 Peter 3:13-14, NLT.

Peter was saying that we likely won't be harmed or hated if we are committed to doing good. But if we're rejected for authentically living out Jesus's brand of radical love, then we can wear such rejection as a badge of honor. However, if we are rejected or hated for the wrong reasons (i.e., for failing to authentically live out the radical love that should be our main identifier), then shame on us.

Consider Mahatma Gandhi's well-known quote: "I like your Christ, I do not like your Christians. Christians are so unlike your Christ." We can either snub the criticisms of our detractors, or we can listen to them. If we find that people are leaving Christianity or struggling with it for the wrong reasons, then we must take responsibility because the New Testament demands it. I believe we've established that the problem is ours and that the solution lies in recovering our brand and then better living it out in a compelling way.

Third, when we are hated, mistreated, rejected, or unjustly criticized, we have a great opportunity to live out our brand in a powerful way. What should make Christianity unique is how we treat our enemies and opponents. As Jesus taught, our job is to love them, bless them, pray for them, and do good to them.[4] In his gospel, Luke gave this challenge: *"If you love only those who love you, why should you get credit for that? Even sinners love those who love them!"*[5] The opportunity to return insults and unfair treatment with Jesus's kind of love is a powerful one.

Listen to what Paul wrote to the Roman Christians who were facing actual persecution:

---

[4] See Matthew 5:43-44, NLT.
[5] Luke 6:32, NLT.

147

Bless those who persecute you. Don't curse them; pray that God will bless them. Never pay back evil with more evil. Do things in such a way that everyone can see you are honorable. Do all that you can to live in peace with everyone. Dear friends, never take revenge. Leave that to the righteous anger of God. For the Scriptures say, "I will take revenge; I will pay them back," says the LORD. Instead, "If your enemies are hungry, feed them. If they are thirsty, give them something to drink. In doing this, you will heap burning coals of shame on their heads." Don't let evil conquer you, but conquer evil by doing good.[6]

When Paul penned these words, the Roman Christians were already facing persecution, but ten years later, they would face a whole new level of challenge in loving those who persecuted them when Nero instituted a severe wave of persecution that imprisoned or brutally killed countless Christians. To provide just one example of how Christians were killed for sport, the Colosseum games featured Christians being wrapped in skins of animals and torn apart by dogs. Throughout the city, Christians were nailed to crosses, covered in pitch, and burned to light Rome's avenues and Nero's outdoor parties. The Roman populace witnessed this brutality, but they also witnessed Christians who chose to turn the other cheek and love their enemies. Forty years later in another wave of persecution, church leader Ignatius encouraged fellow Christians just before his own martyrdom:

Pray continually for the rest of humankind as well, that they may find God, for there is in them hope for repentance. Therefore,

---

[6] Romans 12:14, 17-21, NLT.

allow them to be instructed by you, at least by your deeds. In response to their anger, be gentle; in response to their boasts, be humble; in response to their slander, offer prayers; in response to their errors, be steadfast in the faith; in response to their cruelty, be civilized; do not be eager to imitate them. Let us show by our forbearance that we are their brothers and sisters, and let us be eager to be imitators of the Lord...[7]

As you might imagine, such courageous love in the face of hate did not go unnoticed by non-believers in the empire. Church historians credit such love for enemies as one of the more significant reasons why Christians went from despised to admired. Who loves like that? Jesus people do.

I share this extreme example of persecution from the first century not to compare what we're facing in modern culture to their circumstances, but instead to encourage us to consider our detractors as people to be loved rather than battled. I have been among truly persecuted Christians in various parts of the world, and what we are facing cannot be called "persecution." It's way too early for us to develop a persecution complex.

Yes, we are maligned (and will likely become increasingly so). As Rosaria Butterfield notes, *"Let's face it: we have become unwelcome guests in this post-Christian world. Our children ride their scooters where conservative Christianity is dismissed or denounced as irrelevant, irrational, discriminatory, and dangerous. . . . Christian common sense is declared 'hate*

---

[7] Ignatius, "The Letter of Ignatius to the Ephesians," in *The Apostolic Fathers in English*, ed. Michael W. Holmes (Grand Rapids, MI: Baker Academic, 2006), 99.

speech' by the new keepers of this culture. The old rules don't apply anymore. . . . The language and logic have changed almost overnight."[8]

I have argued that most of our current marginalization is our own fault; we need to be honest about that and be better guests in a post-Christian world. Yet, we will also face unfair characterizations and mistreatment. Christians have always faced these realities. Mistreatment doesn't feel great, but it presents a powerful opportunity to demonstrate grace and love in a way that's hard to dismiss.

So, are we supposed to be liked or hated? The question misses the point, which is that we are to do what Jesus and the apostles commanded: authentically embody the brand of radical love and demonstrate it publicly. As the early church demonstrated, radical love is a powerful and irresistible force. However, not everyone will buy into it—the road may get bumpy, and we may find ourselves being hated anyway. If so, we know what to do: demonstrate radical love to the haters, and by doing so, show ourselves to be honorable.

---

[8] Rosaria Butterfield, *The Gospel Comes with a House Key* (Wheaton, IL: Crossway Books, 2018).

Case Study: Tylenol—Trust Is Everything

The crisis. It all began with a simple headache. In September of 1982, twelve-year-old Mary Kellerman of Elk Grove Village, Illinois, woke up feeling sick, and her parents gave her a Tylenol tablet for her headache. At ten o'clock that morning, she was pronounced dead at nearby Alexian Brothers Medical Center. An autopsy revealed cyanide poisoning. Understandably, her family was in shock. Over the next few days, a total of seven people in the Chicago area died from similar causes. Investigators quickly figured out that all had taken a Tylenol tablet. Testing confirmed that some bottles of Tylenol sold in the Chicago area had been tampered with and laced with huge amounts of Hydrogen Cyanide.

By this point, panic had started to spread, and the story was all over the news as people watched in stunned disbelief. How could a trusted medicine (Tylenol) cause multiple deaths? I remember sitting in the Seattle airport in 1999 and seeing the horror of the Columbine shooting unfold on TV. The entire country was shocked because we never thought that kind of thing would happen here. Just as Columbine dominated the news cycle for weeks, so did the Tylenol poisonings. This was 1982, and the thought of someone deliberately tampering with a product to kill random people was unthinkable. The story dominated the news, and soon the entire country was in shock.

If Tylenol could be poisoned, then how was anything in the grocery store safe to eat?

This is a story about unthinkable human tragedy, but it is also a story about how great brands respond in a crisis—both for their own sake and for the sake of the larger community. Tylenol's response not only saved the brand, but it also transformed the way Americans look at products in the grocery store and re-established trust in the entire system. For the past forty years, this story has been regularly taught in business schools as a textbook example of how responsible companies deal with crises.

The fall. Tylenol was owned by Johnson & Johnson, a 100-year-old company with an impeccable reputation. Millions of Americans trusted their products. Tylenol was the category market share leader with over 35 percent of the market. Then, suddenly, this long-trusted product was found to be killing people. It's hard to imagine today, but people across the US were afraid—not just of Tylenol, but of every product in the grocery store. If this could happen to Tylenol, it could happen to any product.

In an instant, sales of Johnson & Johnson's most profitable product plummeted almost to zero as people lost trust in the brand. Who would buy this product or give it to their family members?

It's important to note that Tylenol was not the only brand losing trust. After all, if Tylenol could be poisoned, then so could any other product in the grocery store. People were freaking out.

The context and the management's mindset. Tylenol generated a lot of money for Johnson & Johnson. In fact, it accounted for nearly 20 percent of the company's total profitability. Shortly after this incident, pundits were already pronouncing that the brand was dead.

On one hand, management knew that they needed to move swiftly and decisively to protect the brand. On the other hand, there were only a few tampered bottles, all of which were in the Chicago area. So, maybe a measured response was more appropriate?

Picture yourself as one of the corporate executives in that board room. You are sitting at the conference table as all of this is presented.

- Your most profitable product is disintegrating before your eyes.

- People are scared to death—not just of your product but of everything in the grocery store. A national panic is affecting far more than just Tylenol sales.

- Remember, it's not your fault. This is not a product quality issue. This is basically terrorism.

As a responsible senior executive, what would you do?

- Do you deflect? This wasn't your fault. Do you react like most political leaders and try to "spin" the story to blame someone else? Do you choose messaging to remind people that this was someone else's fault?

- Or do you stand up and lead in an incredibly bold way, at great cost to your company and shareholders? Do you take immediate responsibility and initiate bold action to make sure that nobody else is injured, regardless of the cost?

To cut to the chase, Johnson & Johnson chose the bold path. A pragmatic response might have been to recall all of their products in the Chicago area, but their trust-based response basically said, "We don't care what it costs. We will leave no stone unturned to fix this."

It all seems very simple in retrospect, but at the time, this was one of the boldest marketing moves ever seen. The company pulled all of its product from store shelves—not just in Chicago, but across the entire country. This amounted to a total of 31 million bottles at a cost of over $100 million (adjusted for inflation, this would amount to nearly $300 million today!). They spared no expense. They even ran TV ads telling people not to take Tylenol, and they offered free replacements for any product already purchased. They offered a reward for the apprehension of people responsible for the tampering.

At some level, Johnson & Johnson functioned less like a brand selling a product and more like a public service protecting the population.

Going beyond. They didn't just remove the current (potentially tampered) product; they took all Tylenol off the market and did not reintroduce it until they had a comprehensive solution in place. The old bottles had a simple cap, but the new bottles had a three-tier system of protection:

- A glued flap on the top of the box to make any tampering immediately evident

- A shrink-wrapped neck seal on the bottle itself

- An inner foil seal that must be broken to access the product inside

These measures immediately changed not just Tylenol but also the entire category. Tylenol went from being the least safe product on the market to being the safest. The triple seal restored trust in the product and the brand, and competitors needed to follow lest they be perceived as unsafe. Tylenol quickly regained its market share (plus more), and the story lives on to this day.

When you walk around the store today and wonder why everything is sealed, the answer comes down to Tylenol and the response they chose over forty years ago. It literally changed the entire grocery store.

The key point here is that the executives at Johnson & Johnson quickly recognized that the public response was not about the product itself. It was a *trust* issue. The tampering incident had eroded trust. Alan Hilburg, a branding consultant who worked with Tylenol's management, put it best: "We concluded we were never going to be judged by what caused the problem. We were always going to be judged on how we responded to it."[9] Tylenol is a great example of how a brand threatened with extinction can recover and even thrive.

What key principles apply to the church?

- **First,** we need to recognize that the brand of Christianity is declining in the US, and the path we're on is not an encouraging one. In 1972, 90 percent of Americans identified as Christian. Today, that number is 64 percent. The fastest growing "religious" group in the US is "nones" (no religious affiliation), which is now up to 30 percent.

- **Second,** we must accept that the decline has resulted from a trust issue. One of the most-often cited reasons for why people reject the church is "Christians not acting like Christians." We get distracted by other things: politics, changing morals, etc. We need to focus on

---

[9] Haberman, Clyde, "How an Unsolved Mystery Changed the Way We Take Pills," The New York Times, September 16, 2018.

displaying the unconditional love and grace of Jesus while recognizing everything else as secondary.

- **Third,** we must avoid making excuses. The media may be biased, but the root cause is not media bias. Morals have changed dramatically over the past fifty years, but the core issue is not about changing morals. The issue is how well we share Jesus's timeless message of love and grace and how well we model (or fail to model) it to a watching world. Let's avoid excuses and focus on the core issue.

- **Fourth,** we need to move decisively and in a way that makes our priorities clear. We can't just be "less mean" or "less political." What would happen if a critical mass of churches in the US took this message to heart and started reaching out to their communities in ways that were undeniably accepting and forgiving? Mother Teresa started by caring for the poor in Calcutta, India, but her actions ultimately changed the lives of millions around the globe.

The actions of Johnson & Johnson restored faith in the Tylenol brand and changed the game for the entire industry. In the same way, a critical mass of Christians can change the game today and restore positive momentum for Christianity in the next generation.

13

WHAT'S AHEAD

"It's tough to make predictions, especially about the future." This quote, which people attribute to everyone from baseball legend Yogi Berra to Nobel Laureate physicist Neils Bohr to an ancient Danish proverb to maybe even my grandmother, holds true regardless of who actually said it first. We've spent much of our time in the last twelve chapters on the past and present, and I would like to end this journey by looking toward the future. With everything going on in American Christianity right now, where do we see this headed? (By "we," I mean the three contributors to this book, each of whom come from different and distinct vantage points.)

Most people I've talked to seem to agree that the American church is at a very significant crossroads, and the next few years are highly critical ones in which Christianity could either gain or lose influence tremendously. We will either recapture our brand internally and then figure out how to connect outsiders to Christ, or we won't. The stakes are high.

Dr. Mark Labberton of Fuller Theological Seminary said, "The Church is in one of its deepest moments of crisis—not because of some election result or not, but because of what has been exposed to be the poverty of the American Church in its capacity to be able to see and love and serve and engage in ways in which we simply fail to do. And that vocation is the vocation that must be recovered and must be made real in tangible action."[1]

With that challenge in mind, the three of us will try to do what is more than a little hazardous: make our own predictions about the future of Christianity in America.

Jeff

By nature, I am an optimist—so much so that I've had to go through counseling to learn how to acknowledge and feel negative emotions. Now that I've completely discredited myself, I do believe that there is every reason to be optimistic about Christianity's future in America. My main reason for optimism is Jesus, who told us what He would be doing between His first and second comings: *"I will build my church and all the powers of hell will not conquer it."*[2] Jesus is always at work in every culture building His church, so I have 100 percent confidence that the church will prevail. Christianity that has stayed true to Jesus by authentically expressing the brand of radical love has survived for two thousand years and will continue to survive until Jesus returns.

---

[1] Wehner, Peter, "The Deepening Crisis in Evangelical Christianity," The Atlantic, July 5, 2019, https://www.theatlantic.com/ideas/archive/2019/07/evangelical-christians-face-deepening-crisis/593353/.
[2] Matthew 16:18, NLT.

Throughout its history, the church has been given a series of significant corrections, and I believe that the American church is due for one. Typically, the emerging generations bring change, and that is my next reason for optimism. When I engage with Gen Z Christians both inside and out of church, I sense God doing a whole new work as those young leaders are capturing the brand more authentically. They see the mission drift and mistakes made by my generation and are committed to expressing the new command in a way that helps people open up to the timeless message of Christianity. They "get it" in ways where I'm still trying to catch up.

I do think that many individual churches and various streams of Christianity may go away completely. Times of massive transition (like now) produce anxiety and fear that cause those infected to make counterproductive mistakes. Remember the fight or flight conversation? In their fear, many Christians and Christian leaders will choose to fight, doubling down on the "us versus them" narrative, and will continue to battle those whom we are called to love. By trying to win, they will lose. Others will choose to flee, retreating to their own variation of a Christian "bubble" that will feel comfortable and likely even successful for a while. With either response, some of those churches and movements will grow for a time as they play on people's fear by seemingly providing a "strong" response. However, the fight or flight of fear will prove to be completely counterproductive, and the next generation (their kids) will almost certainly reject their fear-perverted version of Christianity or reject Christianity altogether. Like a balloon, such churches and movements will expand for a time and then either burst or slowly leak out.

Those who move beyond fear and are open to recovering Jesus's brand and the new things Jesus will do as He continues building His church will find these next years to be both tricky and exhilarating. I hope to be humble enough to listen to the perspectives of critics and those in the next generation that can help bring about a new and fresh expression of the Jesus movement. I would rather be part of the new work Jesus will do through His church than shrink back in fear. That means I'm spending more time with Jesus and more time with younger leaders through whom I believe Jesus will bring about a fresh wind for Christianity in our culture.

I've been in Christian ministry for a long time, and I've never been more excited about the American church's future than I am now. That said, these next few years will be an adventurous ride that is sure to contain significant turbulence.

That brings me to one more cause for optimism. What people in our culture crave in the deepest parts of their souls can only be found in Jesus. If we can live as He empowers us to live, then people will know that He was indeed sent into this world to reconcile people to God and bring the hope and meaning that every soul craves. Like the early church, we will turn our world upside down.

Mike

I really like the analogy at the center of this book—Christianity as a brand—so I will continue in that vein. In my view, Christianity is the ultimate "purpose brand," but it is still a brand that has (at least temporarily) become sidetracked and lost its way. When this happens, one of two outcomes generally follows.

The first possibility is that the brand leaders own the issue and redouble their commitment to the brand's core values. In many cases, this leads to a brand resurgence, causing the brand to become even more influential with its new commitment and energy. To me, this option seems possible but unlikely for the church. I fear that those on the angry side will only dig in deeper and, as Jeff suggested, entire denominations may cease to be relevant. The loudest voices in Christianity, who have been leading the public dialogue for the past thirty years, will soon become irrelevant because they don't reflect the true brand. The next generation is already rejecting this version of the brand.

The second possibility is that the brand does not embrace the need to change and continues to decline. In this case, something else comes along to fill the need that was previously being met by the brand. The need doesn't go away; it just gets satisfied in a different way. For example, when a restaurant or hotel chain declines, another one inevitably takes its place. Sears went away, but now people shop at Target and Amazon. Oldsmobile went away, but Tesla is doing just fine. In my opinion, this is the most likely path for the American church. In its place will come a new kind of church—one that more accurately represents the brand that Jesus established—but it won't be the church as we have known it for the past fifty years.

For years, I have witnessed this decline firsthand, and I have had numerous experiences with genuinely nice people whose only exposure to the church came from people who lead with anger and hypocrisy. I remember when my daughter got her first job as a hostess at a Mexican restaurant near our house. Most of the people she worked with were not churchgoing people. One day, we were talking about

the job and she said, "It's funny. Every Sunday, we get a lot of traffic from the post-church crowd. They're known as being the most
demanding customers and the worst tippers." I remember thinking,
"What a missed opportunity." The very people who could be known
as the kindest and most generous instead behave in a way that leaves
a bad taste in people's mouths.

Like Jeff, I believe that God has specific work for the church to
do. If the most prominent representatives of the church today (let's
say Evangelicals, for the sake of argument) aren't doing it, then He
will raise up others who will. This could come in the form of new
church models, previously lesser-known denominations, etc. But
there will be those who embrace the core message and take it forward.

I'm reminded of the story in 1 Kings 19 in which Elijah is hiding
in the desert, convinced that all of Israel has turned against God,
leaving him as the only faithful one remaining. At Elijah's lowest
point, God appears to him and says that there are actually still seven
thousand people left in Israel who are faithful to Him.

I mention this because we tend to focus on the loudest voices in
Christianity. To be sure, these are the people who define the brand
externally and whom non-Christians see as proof that Christians
don't care. But I see strong evidence of the seven thousand. Many
churches and individuals work faithfully day after day to spread love
and grace in their communities. We certainly don't see them on the
evening news, but they'll be at the center of the coming resurgence.

This book provides one small voice, but my hope is that those
who read it and think likewise can be part of the seven thousand,

and that it will become a movement that reshapes the church's future. Just like the tired and irrelevant church of the 1960s directly led to the Jesus movement of the 1970s, I can see another movement coming that will be championed by the next generation of believers. I can see the dominance of the Evangelical movement waning. Most likely, their brand will continue to decline as this new movement takes its place.

Dwight

What is the future of Christianity in America? If you Google "Christianity in the US," you will quicky find a 2019 article from the Pew Research Center titled "In U.S., Decline of Christianity Continues at Rapid Pace." More recent research from Pew tells us that self-identified Christians make up 63 percent of the population in 2021, down from 75 pecent a decade ago. Additionally, 24 percent of American adults identify as "born-again or Evangelical Protestants," down from 30 percent in 2007.[3]

Let's be clear: if Christianity was a "business," this kind of decline would be seen as calamitous. So, what's going on? What's driving this decline?

I'll begin to address that question by returning to the story I told at the beginning of this book about my dinner with Jeff in 2008 when he told me, "We've been using our power on behalf of the powerful, not the powerless. That's not what Jesus had in mind, was

---

[3] Smith, Gregory A. "About Three-in-Ten U.S. Adults Are Now Religiously Unaffiliated," Pew Research Center, December 14, 2021, https://www.pewresearch.org/religion/2021/12/14/about-three-in-ten-u-s-adults-are-now-religiously-unaffiliated/.

it?" For me, that's the core message of this book. So, let's parse Jeff's thought. What did he mean by "our power," and what did he mean when he suggested using that power on behalf of the powerless rather than the powerful?

Some of the first questions I ask any of my clients are "Where are you advantaged? What are your strengths, and how do you use them to best succeed? In other words, what is the core of your power as a brand, institution, or organization?" This is not a particularly original idea. If you Google "play from your strengths," you'll see a plethora of quotes like, "Don't push your weakness, play with your strengths" or "Find your strengths and play them up."

If "American Christianity" was my client and answered my question about its strengths, my guess is that there would be two points of view.

I'd guess that one point of view would be that "much of evangelicalism's power over the past century has derived, paradoxically, from embracing [the] storyline [that] Evangelicals are the faithful remnant of true Christians, persecuted by secular society for their faithfulness."[4] As one who has little patience with "victimization" and "us versus them" thinking, I'd push back pretty hard against this as a definition of Christianity's core "power."

What would I suggest as the second point of view for defining the core of Christianity's brand? One word: grace. Grace, for me (and remember my "none" status), is the absolute core of Christianity's power.

What is grace? Twentieth century theologian Paul Tillich defined it beautifully:

---

[4] Anderson, Theo, "How Evangelicals Revolutionized U.S. Politics," In These Times, April 12, 2017, https://inthesetimes.com/article/how-evangelicals-revolutionized-us-politics.

Grace strikes us when we are in great pain and restlessness. It strikes us when we walk through the dark valley of a meaningless and empty life. It strikes us when we feel that our separation is deeper than usual, because we have violated another life, a life which we loved, or from which we were estranged. It strikes us when our disgust for our own being, our indifference, our weakness, our hostility, and our lack of direction and composure have become intolerable to us. It strikes us when, year after year, the longed-for perfection of life does not appear, when the old compulsions reign within us as they have for decades, when despair destroys all joy and courage. Sometimes at that moment a wave of light breaks into our darkness, and it is as though a voice were saying: 'You are accepted. *You are accepted,* accepted by that which is greater than you, and the name of which you do not know. Do not ask for the name now; perhaps you will find it later. Do not try to do anything now; perhaps later you will do much. Do not seek for anything; do not perform anything; do not intend anything. *Simply accept the fact that you are accepted!*[5]

For me, the rhetoric of so many churches obscured both the feeling and the power of grace because it felt more like resentment, rage, anger, and power-seeking rather than grace. The words and actions of some of these churches felt (and still feel) hypocritical. Therefore, I believe that the power of this book is found in its hard truths. It speaks directly to my longtime struggle in finding grace that's not obscured by gracelessness.

---

[5] Paul Tillich, The Shaking of the Foundations (Eugene, OR: Wipf and Stock Publishers, 1948).

I have shared the story of my 2008 dinner with Jeff with many people (and remember that I've lived in blue cities in blue states with blue friends). When I tell that story, people are just as surprised as I was. Like many Americans, they are accustomed to seeing Christian leaders be voices of anger, division, and intolerance, so they could scarcely believe that a prominent church leader in Dallas was saying such a thing.

After I tell the story, something curious happens in our conversations: we start to feel hopeful. We're hopeful that we can better listen to each other and that disparate groups of people can move beyond the rancor and rage of our time (as well as the underlying fear and anxiety). We're hopeful that our religious institutions can help fill our world with what we deeply need: the redemptive, resilient, mysterious power of grace and the remarkable feelings of love and gratitude that grace fills us with.

Throughout my career, I've had the privilege of contributing to and even leading some incredible brand turnarounds. In each case, it began with the brand owners looking in the mirror, taking ownership, and recognizing that their actions were not living up to their brand promise. Great brands make promises about things that are deeply important to people and then strive to live up to those promises. The most significant element of a brand turnaround is never the advertising campaign; it's the decision to focus on being faithful to the original promise.

I recognize that the American church has many faces, many of which will continue to seek power for their own ends. However, I am encouraged by what I see in this book. Again, if "the church" was my client, I would say, "Play from your strengths. There's nothing more powerful than grace, so let that be the message that drives your actions, and you will prosper." For me, that's why this book matters.

So, what is the future of Christianity in America? Augustine taught that sin isn't so much an action we take as it is a separation from the Spirit—in simple terms, a separation from grace. This book has documented how Christianity has been seen and experienced by so many—as filled with hypocrisy, anger, and judgement.

Can Evangelical Christianity in America renew its connection to grace? If so, I believe that it will thrive and flourish. Jeff's church has. I hope others do, too.

Jeff

As I mentioned, the three of us have very different perspectives about the future, and only time will tell what the future will hold. Yet, each of us can choose to be far more than passive observers. We are clearly at an inflection point when it comes to the future trajectory of the American church. I am convinced that if Christians are willing to own the problem, take responsibility to recover the brand, and begin to love like Jesus loved, then a spiritually hungry, deeply divided, and overall discouraged world won't know what hit it.

Emerging generations are reacting to an institutional church that lost its distinctive mark. Jesus didn't start a mere institution, however. He launched a movement of radical love. The movement built around Jesus-level love is an irresistible force for good. When it's on-brand, Jesus's church is irresistible. Church history confirms that.

We invite you to join us in this movement. If you would like to be part of the solution of restoring the Jesus brand of Christianity you can do so on our website www.rebrandingchristianity.org. There, you will find podcasts, articles, and other resources to help us all take tangible steps together. You and I are brand ambassadors of the most important brand in history, and so much rides on us getting this right. Yes, we may find ourselves off course at times, but God always invites us back onto the path and helps us to represent His brand well. I believe that now is the time for frank honesty about where we've gone wrong and for laser focus on Jesus's command to love as He loved. Let's join in on God's work of restoring His church and reaching a lost world. As we do, I believe that we will see many people turn toward Jesus in the emerging generations. I can hardly wait! I hope you will join us, too.

ACKNOWLEDGEMENTS

Honestly, I didn't want to write another book. I'd previously written one and gone on the conference speaker circuit at a time when I and a couple of compatriots had something unique to say. It was a unique season, and I believe God used it. Yet, I also resolved that until I had something else unique to say (meaning that there weren't already other people crawling over one another to say the same thing), I was out. Writing a book is too distracting from the passion I have for my own local church.

A few years ago, however, I sensed a nudge from God that became a push. Once again, I had something unique to say. I dragged my feet for as long as I could, but I felt increasingly compelled to write this book that I hope will help spark a movement of people from a variety of Christian flavors who can work together to restore our brand integrity and win over a world to whom we have become unnecessarily repulsive.

Part of my journey involved a sabbatical in which God took over all my agendas for that time. I was unexpectedly overwhelmed with

God's love for me (and you!) in a way that I had never experienced before. It was as if God answered Paul's prayer for the Ephesian church in my own life: *"And I pray that you, being rooted and established in love, may have power, together with all the Lord's holy people, to grasp how wide and long and high and deep is the love of Christ, and to know this love that surpasses knowledge—that you may be filled to the measure of all the fullness of God"* (Ephesians 3:17-19, NIV). I ended my sabbatical determined to do whatever I could to help our church and other churches accurately reflect the heart of Jesus to those He loves. The worst crime we could commit as Christians would be to obscure Jesus's love in a way that pushes away those whom Jesus is urgently passionate to reach. So, I need to thank God for this intervention in my life that has changed me forever. I also want to thank pastor friends like Bruce Miller, Conway Edwards, and Patrick Kelly who helped me process that experience. Add to that list Chase Oakers such as Jack Warren, Glen Brechner, Mark Haun, Paul and Joan Havala, and our board of elders. Thanks to Pete Briscoe, Andy Ho, and Jan Sampeck for pushing me to take the sabbatical in the first place.

A profound acknowledgement must go to Chase Oaks Church for the willingness to be honest, humble, and bold in working to restore our own identity as Jesus's church and pursuing love in the face of misunderstanding and occasional controversy from religious people. Chase Oaks has refused to give into fear that creates an "us versus them" approach. Chase Oakers are amazing.

I also want to thank other churches and leaders around the country who are advancing the conversation and moving the American church forward. The team at the Irresistible Church Network (out of Northpoint Church in Atlanta) has been incredibly helpful and encouraging. Gene Getz, my lifelong mentor, has also cheered me on and offered perspectives from other moments of Evangelical correction in the past.

This book has very much required a team effort. So, thank you to Mariah Swift at The Fedd Agency for keeping the process moving. Thanks also to Ruth Chodniewicz and Brittany Wardie for the incredible edits that made everything better. Greg Holmes and Eric Torrance, pastors at Chase Oaks, also contributed key insights that helped shape the book. My assistant, Lynn French, has wonderfully arranged the interactions of overly busy people to make all this happen.

Mike Hogan and Dwight Jewson, who joined me in the conceptualizing of the book and contributed their insightful case studies, helped this become way more than simply the musings of a pastor. Their perspectives broadened and enriched the entire project, extending beyond the book to the podcast, website, and other forms of media.

I also want to thank my wife, Christy, who has journeyed faithfully with me all these years and has helped keep me going when leading a church gets difficult. Her love for the least and the lost inspires me to keep moving toward the heart of Jesus for His church. My two sons, Collin and Caleb, and their wives, Kenzie and Samantha, also provided fuel and perspective that reminded me to do whatever is necessary to restore our churches as places that can reach the next generation.